TAROT READINGS

BOOK OF COMBINATIONS

VOL 1

Revised 7/18/18

Jennifer E. Reynolds

Copyright © 2014 Jennifer Reynolds

All rights reserved. No parts may be reproduced in any fashion without permission.

ISBN-978-0-9778335-4-2

Copyright
1-6629176556

ROBIN WOOD TAROT – COPYRIGHT ROBIN WOOD ©1991

DECK USED WITH PERMISSION.

Opinions and definitions expressed are those of the author only.

***DEFINITIONS ARE COMPATABLE WITH THE RIDER WAITE DECK

See Tarot Readings: Book of Combinations Vol 2

And Tarot Readings: Layouts

Table of Contents

INTRODUCTION 3
    How to use this book..8
    SIMPLE PHRASES... 11
    BIRTHDATES 15
    MAJOR ARCANA 16
    SWORDS 28
    CUPS 35
    WANDS 42
    PENTACLES 49

TWO CARD COMBINATIONS **56**
    MAJOR 56
    SWORDS 78
    CUPS 92
    WANDS 106
    PENTACLES 120

THREE CARD COMBINATIONS **134**
    MAJOR 134
    SWORDS 157
    Cups 171
    Wands 185
    Pentacles..199

    MEDICAL ASSIGNMENTS 213
    QUIZ 215
INDEX:...223

INTRODUCTION

There is a lot more going on during a reading than just knowing a set of definitions for the cards. There is a shift into a different level of consciousness than your everyday awareness. Your intention becomes focused into something, somewhere out there, where information about what you seek is available. This field of subtle substance whereupon events are impressed is called akasha, ancient Sanskrit word for aether. In Hindu and other language akasha means space or sky. Akashi is a non-physical plane of existence that records every thought, word and action of the human experience but also the history of the cosmos, and enlightenment knowledge.

Other names for this field of information are the collective consciousness, cosmic awareness, and the universal mind. Some people, as Edgar Casey, can tap directly into the akasha records while in a meditative state. Some train to do it using remote viewing. The tarot is just another medium to access this same information. Even the Robin Wood deck is imprinted upon this ether of knowledge along with the energy and definitions for each card. When I (and others) look at and experience a card, we are contributing to the life and energy of its existence in the Akashi field.

An important thing to understand about Tarot is that symbols are being used in the images to impart deep spiritual concepts and teachings. Symbols cross the barriers of language and are therefore universal, much like the use of icons today. The Major Arcana (meaning deep secrets) depicts the soul's journey to enlightenment and the lessons one must learn along the way. The dedicated practitioner of tarot should make a point to study each card and the concepts they represent. Eventually, the symbols will begin to function from the subconscious mind, your higher mind. It is from here that the correct cards are energetically pulled into the readings, completely bypassing the ego of the conscious mind.

Study each card individually, looking at the image as you contemplate its meaning. Try to connect personally with each card. Again, the concepts and emotions of each card need to be imprinted into your subconscious mind because this is how your higher mind is going to be communicating with the universal mind; through the language of the cards. Spend some time handling them, carry them on your body, or sleep with them under your pillow. It is imperative that you imbue your energy into the cards in order to get accurate readings. You will need to do this with each new deck.

Much of the movement of the cards will be happening intuitively and from a higher place, a place outside of time and space. There should be some preparation for connecting to this higher place before you start reading and periodically between readings. To start, I usually hold the cards between the palms of my hands, close my eyes, and take a few deep breaths. I push or connect my energy into the cards. At the same time, I go into a light meditative state. Sometimes I continue to keep my eyes closed as I shuffle, or they are open yet defocused. Either way, I try to remain in this light meditative state as I focus on the information I seek. Instead of trying to bring the information into the conscious mind, where it will be trashed by the ego, the information is allowed to flow directly through me and into the cards. This is like remote viewing in that the information bypasses the conscious mind and goes directly to the pen and paper. The ability to quiet the mind is very helpful, so to improve your ability as a reader it is highly suggested that you practice a form of meditation. Even if you don't have the discipline to mediate consistently, and I don't, a little bit can go a long way.

As you shuffle the deck you are embracing the energy of the deck and the energy of each individual card. In essence, as you shuffle you become one with them. Your energy is flowing through them and their energy is being read, almost as Braille in your hands. Their concepts become the language from which you are reading from the akasha records. The energy of the event from which you are reading will draw, through attraction, the energy of the corresponding cards into the layout. The stronger an event resonates with a particular card, the more consistently that card will appear. You will realize this is occurring when the same card appears in every single layout no matter how many layouts you do, or how short or long you shuffle.

How do you know when to stop shuffling? The best answer is - you don't. It really comes down to intent and trust. You intend and trust that you are stopping at the right time.

Another thing that I personally do, and you don't have to do this, is that after shuffling, I tap the face of the deck two or three times and then I give them a gentle shake before laying them out. While I do this, I am focusing my intention within the heart of the deck for one last energetic connection and to request an accurate reading; that the cards will be arranged as they need to be. Doing so seems to greatly improve the quality of my readings.

Hitting your mark in time and space is kind of like hitting the bull's eye on a dart board. My best readings are when I say, "3 months from now... 6

months from now," or when I say the month and year. Then of course, I focus on that. The closer to an event the more set the outcome is, and hence the more clear and consistent the reading. The further out you get the more opportunity there is for things to change. It's a good idea to continue to check in as time for an occasion gets closer. If you asked, "How's my trip to Hawaii going to be," and it shows you having a wonderful time, but then all of your plans are trashed and fall in ruins. Does that mean the cards were wrong? No. Your trip to Hawaii might be 6 months later and you do have a wonderful time. You only asked to see your trip to Hawaii. Again, it's about hitting the dart board of time and space.

Some people will be easier to read, like an open book. Others readings will be scattered, especially if their life is scattered. Some will even deliberately block you because they are scared or have something to hide – even if they have come to you for a reading.

You are also going to find questions being over-ridden for something much more important or dramatic. Think of events in time and space as having a rector scale. Events with a lot of energy around them are more likely to be picked up. For example, if they are going to be in a car accident but are asking if Johnny likes them, which do you think will more likely show up? Sometimes I say, "Ok. I got that, now how about my first question?" The reading might even be mixed; meaning two events in one layout.

An important thing to keep in mind is that if you hit-on a disaster, especially a death, you could get stuck and NOT be able to read on ANYONE else. For example, I did a reading just to check the next couple of weeks and saw the death of a child (page of cups). This means they are considered by me as a child even if they are in their 20s or 30s. I thought to check on my niece (age 10). She was the first child I read for and it appeared to be her and I believed it to be her. Every reading continued to confirm that it was her. Mistakenly, I didn't bother to read on anyone else. I soon pinned down this death to that weekend, in just a few days. I spoke to her mother and we agreed that my niece should not do a sleep over. Thus decided, I read on my niece and her readings were clear. The problem was that it never was this niece but having talked with her mother, I had unknowingly made a correct connection. By this time, it was late in the evening and seeing her safe, I stopped my readings. That weekend, a distant nephew in another state whom I had no contact with died. It is not likely I could have ever figured out that it was this particular nephew.

You can read the past, all the way back to the beginning of time and you can read on the present, and of course the future. You may be surprised to know that you can read on past lives and future lives, for yourself and others.

World events consistently show up in my own personal readings. I don't know why this happens or if this happens to other readers as well. As yet, I have not been able to determine a distinguishing marker that lets me know if what I am looking at is personal or societal (society). I have mistaken personal readings for societal readings and societal readings for personal readings. For example, I might say, "Me in three months," and get a horrible reading. It turns out to be a social disaster like hurricane Katrina or the Virginia State shooting. I began testing this by doing readings where I ask, "What am I going to be seeing in the headline news in two weeks," and been remarkably accurate. Of course, there are many things you can't know, like what State, or the name of a person.

Some people prefer to keep all cards upright and don't like reading reversed cards. They say there are enough negative cards in the deck that you don't have to do this. I have tried it both ways. If you don't mix your cards then you have to be good at knowing when to take the reversed definition of an upright card. Tarot reading requires a lot of deducing. If you suspect you should be taking the reversed definition of a consistent card, you can try reversing the card and see if you pull it again that way. Sometimes, the cards seem to somehow have reversed themselves! Or, one will pop out at you. Set it aside as you continue to shuffle; it is important to the reading.

There are different ways to shuffle your cards. Shuffling the way you do playing cards, riffling, is going to mix them between upright and reversed. To keep them unmixed, standing the cards on end and shuffling from their sides. Another way to shuffle and keep cards unmixed is to lay the deck on its side. Now pull the deck apart by sliding it in half along the table. See how the cards are still pointed in the same direction? With the card still on the table shuffle ONCE like playing cards (riffing). The technique should be slid, shuffle, slide, shuffle. Just give it a practice and you will see what I mean.

Once you finish laying out the cards, stop and take a moment to look it over. Don't be in a hurry to say, "Ah, I don't get it," and snatch the cards back up to try again. Sure, there will be (few) times when you have totally missed your mark but most of the time, the layouts are correct. You are more likely to go wrong in the interpretation of the cards than to have a bogus layout. Yep, you are going to make mistakes. Even doctors misdiagnose with all their training and high tech equipment. It doesn't mean you aren't any good, so you might as well go ahead and give yourself permission now because even the best still make mistakes.

You are never going to stop learning tarot. I don't know any profession that is stagnate. The cards will continue teaching you something new; a totally new definition, a new combination.

Each layout adds to the puzzle. It is asking too much of 78 cards to be all conclusive in one layout. My average on one subject is 3 to 5 layouts. You will see cards with similar meaning being substituted for each other in consecutive readings. There is always more than one way to say something.

Tarot incorporates mythology, alchemy, astrology, and numerology. No one really knows when the first deck came into being. As close as we can get is that they traveled with the gypsies from the Northern part of India in antiquity before passing through ancient Egypt. They are likely of Hindu origin. At least, that is my conclusion. What is agreed is that they were originally intended to impart spiritual truths and secrete doctrine to the initiate. In the hands of the uninitiated, they became a pallor game and divining tool (a damn good one). The original tarot consisted only of the 22 Major Arcana and were not numbered. The other 4 suits came later and a numbering system was added.

You will find some of the definitions provided in this book to be quite unique. Novices and old-timers alike have exclaimed, *"I never knew you could read tarot this way"*. You will be able to provide yourself and your clients with practical information they can use. A good reader, one who has taken time to perfect this skill, can assist the client with insight and clarity of direction, not to mention the relief gained just from being able to confide in another person who listens to them sympathetically and thoughtfully.

A reputable tarot reader, one who also practices strong ethics and morals, will soon find themselves in high demand.

How to use this book

The best way to use this book is to take a starter deck and write simple phrases. The ones I have provided are just suggestions. Read through the definitions while holding each perspective card in your hand. As you read look back and forth at your card. Spend some time with each– and think. There should be a lot of thinking going on.

After getting a handle on the definitions, card combinations is the next step of learning. I have provided 4 two-card and 4 three-card combinations along with how I would interpret them. That does not exclude all other interpretations but is meant to provide a foundation one can build upon. There are a total of 624 combinations.

These examples are borne out from years of experience. During the process of writing this book, over the course of many years, whenever I would get an interesting read I would make mental note to include it. But, there are so many combination possibilities that all can't be presented.

Medical assignments won't be for everyone but are provided for those who feel comfortable with it and to establish a working hypothesis. If you don't want to use them for others, you can try it for yourself and family. Medical assignments came as a natural inclination because I have been a registered nurse for 18 years. I have read for many nurses and even a doctor and they tended towards asking medical questions. I am comfortable with peppering my readings along medical lines, but I know what I can and can't say. I cannot advise someone to not take their medications, for example, or prescribe them a treatment. What you tell them should be innocuous (harmless). No one should be making major health decisions based upon a reading. You can say they will trip and hurt their leg, or that their child's reading problem is due to difficulty seeing, or that their aging mother is having memory issues. All of these would be okay.

Once, I told a charge nurse that she was going to hurt her leg. Within weeks, she slipped on a melting bag of ice and broke her leg.

One day, my mother called and put me on the phone with her lifelong friend, Mary 'Punkin'. I saw a circulation problem in her neck (World + Hanged Man) and strongly urged that if she felt anything there at all to not ignore it, to not delay, but to seek medical treatment immediately. Unknown to her at the time, she had a growth in her neck and just a few days later while eating she felt something move. She started to ignore it but remembered my warning and had her sister drive her to the hospital. The surgeon said that if she had waited another hour or had turned her head, she would have died within seconds. She actually told the doctor about the reading and he said he believed her because doctors use their intuition all the time. Here is a copy of her letter. It reads in part,

"Thank so much for telling me about my neck. You quite literally saved my life because I would have gone on & turned in first (to bed) & then went to the doctor. My doctor told me that if I had waited for an hour even, I would have died."

In another case, a doctor's colleagues told him that he had bone cancer and advised him to fly home, say his goodbyes and get prepared for what they thought would be chemo and radiation. But, his tarot readings did not show cancer. They showed abdominal problems. He flew overseas and returned for a biopsy. The results were of a benign boney growth but x-ray's revealed dozens of old abdominal stapling's for weight loss.

A sister in another state was having explosive bleeds from her nose. Over time she could feel pressure build up and blood would suddenly spray everywhere, including the dashboard. She was seeing doctors but it wasn't getting better. She sought a reading. I saw that the source was a contaminant in her bedroom, possibly even her bed (4 swords). She was breathing (7 cups) something toxic (devil). She admits she didn't believe me at first but called days later to report that she had decided to turn her mattress over and was more than horrified to find it <u>totally</u> black with mold. Even the sheetrock behind the bed was molded. She learned that the landlord had salvaged the wood framed home from a creek-bed after a flood. She moved out and the nasal bleeding resolved itself. These are just a few examples to give you an idea of how medical assignments can be very beneficial, possibly even saving a life.

Reading for pets is fun and just as accurate as reading for humans. It can be very insightful to find out what these precious souls are thinking. One owner found out that her dog didn't like his food. She objected by saying that she has been giving him the same food for years! She had heard that if you changed their food, it might make them sick. I was dumbfounded and after asking her if she would like to eat the same food every day for years, I suggested she try introducing the new food slowly. So, she went home and mixed the old dog food with the new. She watched the little dog meticulously make two piles. She was thinking the whole while that he was rejecting the new food and could hardly wait to see which pile he would eat. She was surprised when he devoured the new food! It was hilarious. My brother's cat had injured itself but when he picked her up, it hurt so she jumped out of his arms. The reading clearly showed that in her mind he is the one who hurt her. This upset him terribly but he had already suspected she thought this. So he went home and loved up on her. We got our cat from a man with a box of kittens outside of a Krogers. Her reading showed that she thought her mother and siblings were just outside the patio doors. Now we knew why she kept going there. We've had her 12 years now and she is the sweetest cat I have ever had.

So, the best way to use this book is to contemplate the concepts and emotions behind the definitions and behind the combinations. Definitions aren't just words to describe the card. The cards first represent a feeling, a concept, an emotion and words are used later to describe them. The cards aren't imprinted into the ethers as "words", they are imprinted into the ethers as concepts and feelings. So, when you study a card don't just think in terms of memorizing words, ponder what feelings that card would invoke within you and under what circumstances that card would be applicable.

Tarot is fascinating. It is its own language used for more than a millennia to communicate with the unseen field of information all around us. So treat tarot like you would when learning any other language, by serious study – and practice, practice, practice. Once you know the language you can serve as an interpreter between the seen and unseen.

My hope is that this book will shave off years of study by accelerating the learning process though examples.

Simple Phrases

It would be helpful to purchase a practice deck and write a simple phrase on each card until the definitions are committed to memory.

Major Arcana

0 Fool ~ Beginnings.

1 Magician ~ Skilled.

2 High Priestess ~ Secrets.

3 Empress ~ Pregnant.

4 Emperor ~ Authority.

5 Hierophant ~ Religion.

6 Lovers ~ Relationships.

7 Chariot ~ Vehicles.

8 Strength ~ Calm. Pets.

9 Hermit ~ Adviser.

10 Wheel of Fortune ~ Luck.

11 Justice ~ Legal.

12 Hanged Man ~ Limbo.

13 Death ~ Final.

14 Temperance ~ Balanced.

15 Devil ~ Obsession.

16 Tower ~ Ruin.

17 Star ~ Aspiration.

18 Moon ~ Mental.

19 Sun ~ Joy. Birth.

20 Judgement ~ Renewal.

21 World ~ Complete.

22 Blank Card ~ Changeable.

WANDS

Ace Wands ~ Creative.

2 Wands ~ Goals.

3 Wands ~ Business.

4 Wands ~ Marriage.

5 Wands ~ Worry.

6 Wands ~ Admired.

7 Wands ~ Success.

8 Wands ~ Progress.

9 Wands ~ Defensive.

10 Wands ~ Hard work.

Page Wands ~ Announce.

Knight Wands ~ Travel.

Queen Wands ~ Socialite.

King Wands ~ Charismatic.

SWORDS

Ace Swords ~ Analytical.

2 Swords ~ Decision.

3 Swords ~ Injury.

4 Swords ~ Rest.

5 Swords ~ Trouble.

6 Swords ~ Trip.

7 Swords ~ Criminal.

8 Swords ~ Trapped.

9 Swords ~ Pain.

10 Swords ~ Ruined.

Page Swords ~ Urgent.

Knight Swords ~ Rescue.

Queen Swords ~ Healer.

King Swords ~ Soldier.

CUPS

Ace Cups ~ Love.

2 Cups ~ Agree.

3 Cups ~ Celebrate.

4 Cups ~ Disappointed.

5 Cups ~ Grief.

6 Cups ~ Kids.

7 Cups ~ Imagination.

8 Cups ~ Leaving.

9 Cups ~ Happy.

10 Cups ~ Family.

Page Cups ~ Child.

Knight Cups ~ Romance.

Queen Cups ~ Mother. Wife.

King Cups ~ Father. Husband.

Pentacles

Ace Pentacles ~ Money.

2 Pentacles ~ Exchanges. Deliberating.

3 Pentacles ~ Job.

4 Pentacles ~ Possessive.

5 Pentacles ~ Illness.

6 Pentacles ~ Giving or Receiving.

7 Pentacles ~ Laborer.

8 Pentacles ~ School.

9 Pentacles ~ Affluence.

10 Pentacles ~ House.

Page Pentacles ~ Payments.

Knight Pentacles ~ Loan.

Queen Pentacles ~ Ethnic female.

King Pentacles ~ Savings.

Birthdates

Write birthdates on an index card and keep with your deck.

King & Queen of Swords: Aquarius. Gemini. Libra.

King & Queen of Pentacles: Virgo. Capricorn. Taurus.

King & Queen of Wands: Aries. Leo. Sagittarius.

King & Queen of Cups: Pisces, Scorpio, Cancer.

Aries - March 21 to April 20

Taurus - April 21 to May 20

Gemini - May 21 to June 20

Cancer - June 21 to July 22

Leo - July 23 to August 22

Virgo - August 23 to September 22

Libra - September 23 to October 23

Scorpio - October 24 to November 22

Sagittarius - November 23 to December 21

Capricorn - December 22 to January 19

Aquarius - January 20 to February 19

Pisces - February 20 to March 20

Tarot Readings: Book of Combinations

Definitions

Major Arcana

0 THE FOOL: New beginning. Childlike. Youthful. Naive. Gullible. Unaware. Vulnerable. Trusting. Innocence. Not guilty. A virgin. Pure. Untouched. Unadulterated. Chaste. Fidelity. Not cheating. Brand new. Newer or younger. The younger generation. Not experienced or done this before. Optimistic. Lack of concern. Lack of foresight. Thoughtless. Unaware of it or knows nothing of it. They are innocent or are found innocent. Oblivious to the fact. Unseen perils. Not enough experience to be wary of dangerous situations.

THE FOOL: (Reversed) Foolish act. Unwise decision. The sensation of feeling stupid or foolish. They feel the other person in question did a stupid thing. A mental or physical disability or mental or physical handicap. Adult with a child's mentality. Mentally slow. Poor or low IQ. They can't read or write. Uneducated. Simpleton. Weak minded. Careless. Easily coerced. Awkward. Clumsy. Crude and uncouth. Many times this card can be upright and still mean its reversed definitions.

1 THE MAGICIAN: An adept. Mastery in their chosen profession or craft. A professional or expert. Skilled. Shows ability. Knowledgeable. Natural. A rugged, earthy man who is virile, potent, charismatic, handsome. A man with a beard. Generational and ancestral lineage and reincarnation. Shaman type person. A naturalist. Herbalist. Learned in natural or holistic healings. Belongs to Hermetic order, Freemasons, or Knights Templar or similar sacred societies.

THE MAGICIAN: (Reversed): Not capable or skilled in their profession or craft. Lacks experience or expertise. Lacks the talent or aptitude. Having self-doubt or feeling inept in their abilities. An object inferior in some way or of poor craftsmanship. Shoddy or sloppy work. Using magic to harm others. Black magic (even if card is upright). Being involved in satanic activity. A hex or curse has been performed.

2 HIGH PRIESTESS: Secret. Hidden information. Private, or personal information. Confidential. Classified. Top secret. Database. Stored information. Mystery. Mystical. Mysterious. Psychic intuition. An individual (male or female) with spiritual gifts of insight and intuition. They may be clairvoyant, clairaudient, or a combination of both. Psychic activity happening. Initiations and secret societies. Spiritual person or teacher. You will get this if reading for another psychic or can show up for the reading or reader them self. She is Isis, the aethers, the quantum field, the Akasha records. She is the unseen creative force in the universe. The magi (Magician) draws upon her to create matter in the physical realm. She is the holy spirit called Shekinah.

HIGH PRIESTESS: (Reversed) Disclosing confidential, private or personal information. Telling a secret. Gossiping. Snitch. Whistle blower. Lacking intuition, insight or knowledge. Self-conscious. Shyness. Is against psychic abilities or practices. Misuse of knowledge, whether they are exposing a secret or hiding something. Wrong use of psychic powers. Psychic attack.

3 THE EMPRESS: Maternity. Pregnancy. A baby. One's mother or mother figure. A matriarch in the family. A wise older female. Elder relatives; grandparents, aunts and uncles. Nurturer or care giver of children or the elderly. Baby sitter. Baby-sitting. Daycare center. Retirement home or nursing home. Medical: Abdominal problems: stomach, gallbladder, pancreas, uterus, other female organs.

THE EMPRESS (reversed): Having a problem with their mother or elders. Difficulty getting pregnant or with the pregnancy. Losing the baby. Miscarriage or abortion. Childless. Being sterile. On birth control pills. Having a hysterectomy. Don't want children or has a fear of parenting. A bad or negligent parent, grandparent, or babysitter. Babysitting problems. Having no parental supervision. A smothering mother. The baby, mother, or an elder is sick. Problems in stomach area or gynecological problems (as upright card).

4 THE EMPEROR: Having a high position (man or woman) or in a position of authority. The owner, boss, or president of a company. Directors and CEOs. Any official organization or department. Human resources. A powerful, virile leader. A President. A dictator. An Official. Having legal authority. Power of attorney. District attorney. Immigration authority or officer. Having dominance over others. A person who's decisions would be purely business and not based on emotion. A stern individual. Bossy, controlling, dominating, aggressive person (even if upright).

THE EMPEROR (Reversed): Stubborn. Dominating. A bully. An obstinate, arrogant and controlling male or female. Lacks emotional concerns. Abuse of power. Loss of a position of power or control over others, or over a situation. Oppressive individual. Lacking restraint in aggression. Being at odds with the established order. Others trying to control you. Dry season. Drought.

5 THE HIEROPHANT: Religious. Place of worship (Church. Temple. Mosque. Synagogue. Monastery. Orphanage, Catholic school). Prayers. God in their life. Spiritual authority (Chaplain. Reverend. Preacher. Minister). A ceremony. A ritual. A thing of tradition. "It's our policy". A traditional institution, department, or organization. Being different. Eccentric. A person of a different color, race, religion, or culture. A homosexual, gay. Foreigner. Alien being.

THE HIEROPHANT (Reversed): Actions that are irregular and go against tradition. They are gay. Feeling shut off from God or that prayers aren't answered. Abandoning a previous belief system or religion. Anti-religious. An atheist. Dogmatic. Fanatical. Hypocrite. Unethical or immoral. A foreign religion or social structure. A couple has social, cultural, racial, or other differences. Person of a different race, religion, or Country. For example, if client is white then the individual in question could be black or Hispanic, If client is black, then individual in question could be white, etc.' An illegal alien. Alien activity as in "aliens".

6 THE LOVERS: A couple who are romantically or sexually involved. Healthy or good relationship and partnership. Well suited for another. Working towards a common goal. Being on the "same page" as another. Equanimity. They complement or balance each other's attributes. A male and a female both. In a health reading represents the reproductive organs including breasts and sex organs. Anything transmitted from person to person whether sexually or not. Even upright can mean sexual abuse.

THE LOVERS (Reversed): The relationship splits up. Having an argument with your partner. It isn't a good relationship. Being mismatched. Growing apart. Unfaithfulness. Cheating. Having an affair with a married or otherwise committed person. A sexually transmitted disease. Any communicable or transmittable, contagious disease regardless of sexual activity. Nudity. Problems with sexual organs (breasts, uterus, penile, prostate). An aberration in sex. Sex addiction. Sexual abuse. Rape. Prostitution. Sexual predator. A pedophile. Impotent. A sex change. A transvestite. Same sex partners.

7 THE CHARIOT: Control. Able to control the direction of a situation. A control issue. A vehicle. At a literal level, the Chariot represents all means of transportation. An automobile. An airplane. A boat. A motorcycle. Even a bicycle, tricycle, scooter, skates, or wheelchair. An actual horse and carriage. Transportation. Trafficking. Metaphysically, having good control of ones ego personality and emotions.

THE CHARIOT (Reversed): Having no control over a situation. It's not in your control. Car problems. Car breaks down. Car is stolen, repossessed or towed. Having no car. Losing control of a vehicle. A crash or wreck of any type of vehicle. Transportation problems.

8 STRENGTH: Having inner strength, fearlessness and courage. Having a calming effect on others. A humanitarian. Peacemaker. Healer. Having a healing touch. Having great empathy and understanding. Perseverance. Leading by a gentle persuasion of feminine energy. Read literally, any animal (wild or domestic). Large animals (horses, cows). Small animals (cats, dogs, rats, birds). Bugs (roaches, fleas, mosquitoes). Having parasites. Having allergies or being allergic. Someone who works with animals. A veterinarian. A animal trainer or groomer. They are afraid.

STRENGTH: (Reversed): Having an infirmity. Feeble. Weak. Malaise. Fatigued. Tired. Fear. Fearful. Afraid. Phobia. Panicked. Panic attacks. Coward. Problem with an animal. Animal abused or injured. An animal attacks. Microbiological agents or organisms; including bacteria, spores, viruses, parasites. Chemical or biological agents. Unable to control things around you. This is one of several cards that can be upright or reversed and represent a problem.

9 THE HERMIT: Having found enlightenment, he or she sheds Light for others. A Counselor. Contract worker or advisor. A leader. A Guide. Seer. Mentor. Guru. Teacher. Giving or receiving guidance. A seeker of truth. Seasoned. Wise person. Therapist or clergy. Spiritual awareness. Looking. Searching for someone or something. A tracker. Bounty hunter. To investigate. Background check. To discover. To expose. Anything used to see, such as glasses, microscope, a light, a telescope. Under surveillance. A surveillance camera. The NSA. A tracking device. GPS device or signal. The 'black box'. Medically: Visual problems. Old age. Senior citizen. Elderly person. Something (anything) that is old or aged (like expired food). Solitude. Reclusive. Isolation. The Winter months.

THE HERMIT (Reversed): Poor advice. Being misled. Being lost or just feeling lost. Unable to find someone or something. A loner. Withdrawn from society. A situation is not investigated. A thing is not or was not visible. Not under surveillance. Not watched. Seeks to hide the truth or is avoiding the truth. Hiding something or some "thing". A hidden agenda. Being kept in 'the dark'. The deceased is not in the Light. Losing one's spiritual way. Problems with lighting or being able to see. Vision or eye problems. Cataracts. Needs glasses. Blindness. Eye injury, eye infections or lazy eye. Nighttime.

10 WHEEL OF FORTUNE: Good fortune. Good luck. Lucky for you or in your favor. An inheritance. The situation turns around for the better. Winning. Gambling. Lottery. Some action you have taken will bring good fortune. Making lots of money. A windfall. Summer months.

WHEEL OF FORTUNE (Reversed): A reversal of fortune. Things are not in your favor. Being unlucky. Misfortune. Losing the gamble. Bankruptcy. Not getting the inheritance. Winter months.

11 JUSTICE: The legal system. Legal matters. Legal authority. Any governmental department or office. Court systems (criminal, juvenile, child protective). Fairness. Balance. Justice. Action is justified. Right decision. Equality. Unbiased. Doing the right thing. Rational thought. Negotiations. Anything legal; certification, licensing, tests, contracts. Discerning the truth. A specific technology. Science. Research. They are in politics. Legal professions: lawyer, Judge, jury, mediator, bail bondsman. School testing or medical testing.

JUSTICE (Reversed): Legal problems. Having the judgment go against them. Being sued. Delays in legal matters. Being penalized. Losing your license or certification. Licensing or certificates revoked. Failing a test. Not passing the boards. Discrimination. An injustice done. Treated unfairly. Biased. Showing prejudice. Harassment. It is not legal. Incrimination. Dirty politics.

12 THE HANGED MAN: In limbo. Things are on pause. Suspended physically. Delays. Postponing gratification. Sacrifice for others or for a higher good. Betting suspended such as from work or school. Seeking truth or inner vision. Piercing the veil. Raising one's consciousness. Having visions. Remote viewing. Meditation. An inter-dimensional Being. Astral travel, OBE. Being visited by a spirit. Having a spirit attachment. Presence of a disembodied consciousness. An entity. Alien activity. Depending on surrounding cards, can mean a serious situation, accident or injury that threatens life. Life hangs in the balance. Incapacitated. Problems or injury iin head, neck, or throat areas. Hung. Choked. Suffocated. Strangled. Beheaded. Drowned. Something that bites or stings. A bee, snake or spider.

THE HANGED MAN (Reversed): The reversed is much like the upright. Choking. Strangled. Suffocating. Vomiting and aspirating. Drowning. Read literally: Death by hanging. Beheaded. Negative influences of a spirit attachment. Sacrificing one's life or own dreams for the benefit of others. Problem or injury in the head, neck, or throat areas. A major injury or trauma. Someone who is very ill and suffering. Their life hangs by a thread; it could go either way. Almost as ominous as the 3 of Swords.

13 DEATH: Dramatic change. The original path is blocked and one is forced to take a different path. A profound transition or transformation. The end of one era and the beginning of another. Pursuing a dead end. Something is finished. Final. The end. It's over. The death of a career, business, or relationship. The action or activity is being blocked. Rarely means actual death unless surrounding cards support such a scenario. The presence or message from a dead person. Medically: Menopause. Necrosis (decay). Gangrene.

DEATH (Reversed): Staying in a situation they should not. Continuing down the wrong path. Resistance to change. Stuck in old habits. Stagnation. In a rut. Gotten all they can out of a situation. No growth occurring. No changes made. Going into remission. Something going on for a very long time (good or bad). Death will not occur as feared. Can indicate that a person is not actually dead. They survived a near death experience. Does not recognize they are dead. Medically: the word 'chronic'. In a dormant state. Is in remission.

14 TEMPERANCE: Balance. Stability. Organized. Coordination. Synchronizing. Patience. A thing being in a process. Running smoothly. Transformation. Manifesting. In due time (the wheels are turning). Bringing things to pass. They can do anything. They can make things happen. Having flow. Doing the right thing at the right time. Functioning from their higher self. Being highly evolved spiritually. Working with the higher realms and angels. Divine intervention or protection. One's Spirit guide or Guardian Angel. The object in question is made of metal. Metallurgy (gold, silver, copper).

TEMPERANCE (Reversed): Unable to cope. Feeling overwhelmed with the situation. Stressed and burnt out. Feeling off balanced. A thing out of balance. Uncoordinated. Impatient. Lack of flow. Working against the Light.

15 THE DEVIL: Obsession. Compulsion. Greed and corruption. Drug addiction (prescription or not). Perversion of desire, lust, appetite, excess. Obsessive-compulsive behaviors or habits. Of a negative influence. Negative energy or entity. The dark side. Anything bad for you: drugs, alcohol, caffeine, smoking, overeating, sexual deviations. Abusive or harmful relationships. Anything toxic for you. Actual toxins (chemical, gases, poison, pollutants, pesticides, rotten, contaminated purulent, infected).

THE DEVIL (Reversed): Breaking free from a drug or alcohol addiction, an obsession, or a bad habit. Releasing oneself from any negative situation or toxic relationship. Letting go of attachment to material possessions or of negative emotions. Freeing oneself from an evil influence. Working against dark energies: light Worker, Reiki, healing touch. Clearing negative energy.

16 THE TOWER: Ruin and devastation. Disaster. Catastrophic event. Chaos. Swift and dramatic event. Violent weather such as represented in the card (earthquake, lightning, flood, tornado, fires, drought, hurricane, mud slide, typhoon, tsunami). Forces beyond one's control. Broken relationships. Loss of property. Bankrupt. Disgrace. Loss of one's status in life. A great investment of time and effort now crumbles to ruins. Having a major crisis. Beware if you are seeing this card in several client's readings and your own. It could foretell of a disaster to occur, either locally or of a global consequences; especially if in the environment position.

THE TOWER (Reversed): Narrowly escaping a disaster. A crisis is averted. A crisis is now over. Having come through a harrowing time. A lesser devastation or lesser dramatic event than could have occurred. Having missed being involved in a severe weather situation. What was once a disaster isn't such a disaster any longer or a bad situation is reversed.

17 THE STAR: Hopes and wishes. Aspirations and dreams. Bright prospects. Spiritual growth. Achieving a cherished goal. Attainment. Obtaining what they want in life. An astrologer or astronomer. Something from the sky. Not of this world. The alien abductee card (so is Hierophant card). Spring time. Nighttime.

STAR: (Reversed): Dashed hopes and dreams. Not achieving one's goals or desires. Unsuccessful. Let down or disappointment. An expectation went unfulfilled. Lack of inspiration or motivation. Lost all hope or promise. An end of their career. Something falls or "comes down from" the sky. Asteroid or Meteorite. Plane crash. UFO.

18 THE MOON: The subconscious mind. Psychic activity. Could mean to trust your instincts and intuition. Confused as how to proceed. Because of the moon's magnetic pull, which affects the tides, it also affects us mentally so indicates a multitude of mental disturbances, breakdowns and psychosis. Feeling restless. Mental strain. Mentally unstable. Scattered thought. Unable to concentrate. Memory loss. ADHD. Sundowners. TIA's, Amnesia. Dementia. Alzheimer's. Being unconscious. Coma. The moon's glow is just a reflection and hence the traditional meaning of a warning of illusion and deception. The actual moon. Medically it represents anything round; tumors, cysts, growths, etc.' Nighttime.

MOON (Reversed): All upright definitions but worse. Mentally disturbed. Things aren't what they seem. Misperceiving. Mental disorders. Stroke. Psychotic break or episode. Paranoia. Schizophrenia. Hallucinations.

19 THE SUN: Happiness. Jubilation. Enthusiasm. A sense of freedom and feeling uninhibited. Contentment. Having no troubles. The birth of a child. Pregnant. A baby. Could mean it is their birthday. Having a bright, sunny personality. Feeling young and vibrant. Playing in the sun. At the beach. Taking vacation at a sunny location. Sunbathing. Indicates temperatures and extremes of heat. Summer months. Daytime.

THE SUN (Reversed): Being unhappy. Depression. Having an unpleasant, disagreeable disposition. Getting too hot. Sun-stroke. Sun burned. Fever. Dehydration. Drought. A thing gets over heated. Seasonal Affective Disorder (SAD). Winter months. Sometimes, getting this card upright can still mean its reversed definition of depression. Always consider a card's reversed meaning as being a possibility.

20 JUDGEMENT: Attainment. Great success. Victory. Realization. Triumphant. Overcoming adversity. Coming through a time of tribulation (i.e. 'through the fire'). Absolution (vindicated) and redemption. Being in good physical health. Physically fit. Good stamina. A trim or muscular body (the 6-pak abs). Being revitalized, re-energized. Getting physical therapy, a chiropractor, acupuncture. Purified and cleansed. Regaining one's health. Making a full recovery. Anything to do with the physical body. Dance. Yoga. The gym. Exercising. The naked body. A stripper. A thing has been refurbished and is like new. Rejuvenation and rebirth. Reincarnation.

JUDGEMENT (Reversed): Poor health. Does not recover or regain one's health. Is not rejuvenated. Physically unfit. Body (or item) is in poor condition. Feeling run down and tired. Unable to be restored to its original form and function.

21 THE WORLD: Completion. Encompassing all. The whole. Attainment of desire. Self-actualization. Reached a major goal. The ultimate (of anything). An epitome. Triumphant. Limitless. Infinite. Universal or world-wide. International. A multinational. Indicates another State or city. Transcontinental flight. Overseas or Interstate travel. From another Country. A collective whole (everyone, everything). Not earthbound. Anything above the earth. Airplane. Drone. Satellite. Space shuttle. UFO. Circles the earth. Upper atmosphere. The end of the journey begun by the Fool. As a health card: their circulation. In the case of cancer, means metastasized.

THE WORLD (Reversed): Feeling incomplete or unfulfilled. A thing or act is not completed. Having not reached their goals. It ain't over (in regards to a relationship or situation). Falls to earth. Down from above. Losing altitude. Flight problems or delays. No interstate travel is allowed (for legal reasons). Airplane crash. The soul is earthbound.

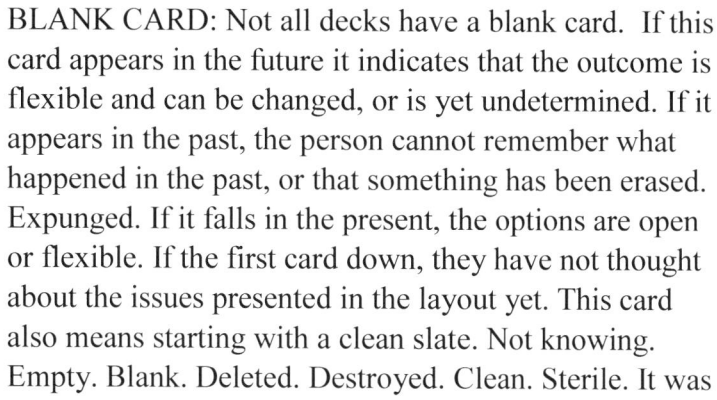

BLANK CARD: Not all decks have a blank card. If this card appears in the future it indicates that the outcome is flexible and can be changed, or is yet undetermined. If it appears in the past, the person cannot remember what happened in the past, or that something has been erased. Expunged. If it falls in the present, the options are open or flexible. If the first card down, they have not thought about the issues presented in the layout yet. This card also means starting with a clean slate. Not knowing. Empty. Blank. Deleted. Destroyed. Clean. Sterile. It was removed. Disappeared. Not there. It never happened. It didn't or won't occur. Destruction of evidence. Having no clues. Having no evidence. They do not know anything about it. Having no plans. Clear conscious. If your deck didn't come with a blank card, you can make one by gluing a blank paper to any extra card that came with the deck.

Before we proceed, it should be said that sometimes not getting an expected card in the layout is just as significant. For example, they want to know if their lover is cheating but you don't get a 7 of Swords, or a reversed Lovers card, or a reversed Knight of Cups, etc.' In this case, you would say, *"I don't see anything that indicates that they are cheating"*.

Another thing to point out is that there is no hard and fast rule that you have to take the upright definition of a card if it falls upright. The better way to read is to be flexible while going through a type of mental gymnastics as you consider surrounding cards to determine which definitions might apply. You will find that learning tarot improves your mental agility and problem solving skills in your everyday life.

Swords

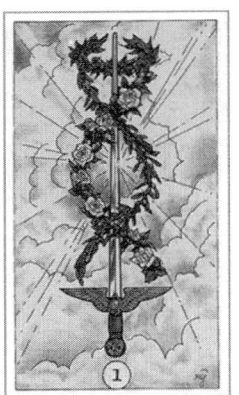

ACE OF SWORDS: Success. Victory. Attainment. Knowledge. Technology. The answer is yes. Absolutely. Positively. Positive attitude. Positive thinking. Inspirational. A good outcome to any endeavor. Clarity of thought. Sharp mind. Intelligent. Analytical process. Strategic. Brilliant. Very bright. Read literally, any sharp object or sharp pain. Swords mean knowledge but also encompass the whole of war and peace. They are in the Light. Positive energy (white Light). Spiritual.

ACE OF SWORDS (Reversed): Negative thinking. Negative attitude. Over judgmental. Criticizing. Faultfinding. Nitpicker. Contradicting person. Discouraging individual. Confrontational. A hostile person, environment, or situation. Mental frustration and tension. Over thinking. Over analyzing. A poor strategist. Big fight. Declaration of war! The reversed Ace of Swords came up for the event of 911.

2 OF SWORDS: Decision. A choice between two things or actions. Careful consideration. Setting priorities. The number 2 is the number of duality, balance, and choice. An important choice or decision has to be made. This card is about personal changes or it was (or is) a crossroads in their life. Things have changed. Changes were made (to it). Took it in a different direction.

2 OF SWORDS (Reversed): Making a wrong choice or wrong decision. Cannot choose or refusing to choose or make a decision. Not knowing how to proceed or address an issue. It is not their choice or decision to make.

3 OF SWORDS: Tragedy! Serious injury or accident. Sudden illness. Death. Murder. Suicide. Hatred. Kill. Die. Shot. Stabbed. Cut. Bleeding. Divorce! Separated from. Severance. Fired! Quitting! Heartbreak. Emotional pain. Heart attack. Heart surgery. Severed artery. Stroke. Hemorrhage. Any surgery. Needle stick. IV drug user. Tattoos. The definitions this card could cover are almost endless, anything that cuts, punctures, pierces, or causes physical injury. This is the most dramatic card and means death more often than the death card. It is highly recommended that if you get this card that you pursue it so that the event might be avoided, and it very well can be.

3 OF SWORDS (Reversed): Still serious but less dramatic when reversed. Does not commit suicide or murder. Does not die. Is not killed. Heartbreaks, injuries, and surgeries are less severe. Having a crisis intervention.

There are 5 cards that if seen together in a reading can indicate actual death. The 3 of swords, 5 of cups (grief), 9 of swords (tears), Tower card, and least of all, the death card. The death card is not about death but about endings and transformations. At least 3 of these should be present to even suggest a death. Unfortunately, the 3 of swords alone can mean death, serious life threatening accident or surgery. But if also present with death card is the 5 of cups or 9 of swords, or tower card, then death is much more likely and should at least be gently presented as a possibility. Many just want to hear good things, but if you don't mention it and something does occur they will question why you didn't catch it. You could start by asking, *"If I see something bad, would you want me to tell you about it?"*

4 OF SWORDS: At rest. Relaxation. Recuperation. Recovery time. Vacation. Time off. A leave of absence. A period of introspection. Meditation. Hypnosis. Being on bed rest (as during pregnancy). Bedridden. Sleep. A bed. A bedroom. Being at peace. Having peace of mind. Taking it easy. Not working. Just being lazy. "No sweat". It doesn't bother them in the least.

4 OF SWORDS (Reversed): Not getting enough rest or sleep. Sleeping too much. Sleep disorders. Insomnia. Sleep apnea. Narcolepsy. Not resting well or not feeling rejuvenated. Feeling tired. Drowsy. Lethargic. No free time. Needs a vacation or a break. Vacation is interrupted or postponed. Doesn't have a bed. No place to sleep.

5 OF SWORDS: Trouble. Difficulties. Cheater! Trickery. Sneaky. Sly. Deceit. Liar! Stealing. Treachery. Deception. Betrayal. A ruse. A gimmick. An imposter. Phishing. A sceme. Taking advantage of others. Winning by unfair means. Gossip. Mocking. 'Back stabbing'. Watch your back. Taking another's credit for something that is not theirs. Deliberate effort to defeat or do harm to an endeavor. Undermining a project. Picked on. Bullying.

5 OF SWORDS (Reversed): They are trying to take advantage of another but aren't getting anywhere. Thwarting or diverting an attempt by another to do harm.

6 OF SWORDS: Taking a trip by road, plane, or over water. Someone journeys to see you or you to see them. Being from out of State. Leaving troubles behind. Situation improves. Tensions ease. Their destiny. An actual boat or ship.

6 OF SWORDS (Reversed): Trip canceled or delayed. Having to take a trip that is objectionable or that one loathes to take. Something has gone wrong with the trip. Actions are taking you into troubled waters. Losing the trail. Thrown off the track. Going the wrong way. Read literally, going back the way they came. They return or circle back. Upright or reversed, someone may be scoping out your house or work such as doing drive-by's to check it out. Look for other trouble cards.

7 OF SWORDS: A criminal. Criminal activity. Illegal. An illegal alien. Stealing. Robbery. Intruder. Infiltrator. Treachery. Betrayal. Sabotage. Malice intent. Conspiracy. Kidnapping. Being stalked. Fraud. Stolen identity. "Cat-Phishing". Extortion. Adultery. They are cheating. Drug dealing. Spying. Private investigator. A spy or double agent. Cunning. They are guilty. Being paranoid. Being secretive. Being suspicious. Covers all negative human emotions and actions. Covers all criminal activity and any covert governmental activity.

7 OF SWORDS (Reversed): Same as upright meaning but adds the element of deception and subterfuge, not an "in your face" kind of criminal. It's a gimmick or scam. Ponzi scheme. Double-dealing. 'Cooking the books'. An imposter. A ruse. A trick. Being fleeced. Being 'taken-in' or being manipulated. A habitual criminal. A career criminal. A predator. A stalker.

8 OF SWORDS: Trapped. Restricted. Hindered. Prohibited. Restrained. Restraining order. Inhibitions. Committed. Obligated. The prison or jail card. Someone will be going to jail or is in jail. Detained. Child grounded. Locked in. Fear of commitment. Loss of freedom or free time. Inaction through fear. Read literally, tied up. Kidnapped. Captive. Forced. For pets; a cage, their carrier, collar, or harness. A fence. Indicates a soul is earthbound.

8 OF SWORDS (Reversed): Freedom! Escaping. Untied. Unrestrained. Loose. Released from jail. Refuses to be tied down or obligated to a job, project or relationship. Free from inhibitions. Medically: Respiratory ailments. COPD. Emphysema. Asthma. Pulmonary fibrosis. Lung cancer, especially if with Knight of Swords (cancer). Congested. Chronic cough. Bronchitis. The flu. Broken rib. Crushed chest. The soul is free from the physical body. The soul is not earthbound.

9 OF SWORDS: Tears. Crying. Feeling hurt. Emotional upset. Mental anguish. Troubles and woe. Reliving past injuries. Actual physical pain. Fibromyalgia (pain syndrome). Nightmares. Bad dreams. Night terrors.

9 OF SWORDS (Reversed): Coming through a time of emotional pain or physical suffering. Getting pain relief. No more crying. Anguish is over. Having mentally worked through issues that were once causing distress and heartache. It wasn't painful, or was not in pain.

10 OF SWORDS: Devastated! Totally ruined. Major betrayal. Stabbed in the back. Victimized. Martyrdom. Completely drained and depleted of all energy, or motivation. Drained of their resources. Feeling exhausted. Letting others exhaust your time and energy. Medical: Bleeding out. Free bleeder. Bled to death. Anemia. Ruptured spleen. Broken back. Vertebrae problems. Ruptured discs. Metal plates, shrapnel, or pins in the back. Prosthetics. Heavy metals in the body: mercury, lead, nickel..

10 OF SWORDS (Reversed): Overcoming devastation. Refusing to be victimized or taken advantage of anymore. Resentment of prior mistreatment. Using your energies and resources wisely. Bone, back, or vertebra problems.

PAGE OF SWORDS: Urgent, exciting, or alarming and unexpected news! A sense of urgency. Hearing of problems and difficulties, maybe even learning about it on the news or in newspapers. Unconventional (risky or dangerous) activity. Swiftness. All of a sudden. A very active, alert, fast moving, intelligent child. Hyperactive behavior. A youth (male or female) born in air sign (Aquarius, Libra, Gemini). A young soldier. A youth with a weapon. A male child if question is of gender (even though all Pages in this deck are girls).

PAGE OF SWORDS (Reversed): Behavioral problems in a child (or an immature adult). They are irrational, undisciplined. Their behavior is out of control. They are impatient, inconsistent, unpredictable, possibly even hostile. Hyperactive child. An errant, wayward troubled child.

KNIGHT OF SWORDS: Heroic. Coming to the rescue. Police officer. Fire fighter. Security guard. Ranger. Medical emergency personnel or paramedic. FEMA. Red Cross. Defender of truth and justice. Righteous anger. Noble action. Armed. Carries a weapon for use in their profession. Mounting a defense. An attack. Many times this card takes its reversed definition even though it is upright.

KNIGHT OF SWORDS (Reversed): Very angry! Violent action. Weaponry. Guns or knives. Unregistered or illegal firearms. Radical behavior. Dishonorable. Dishonesty. Can mean a lack of courage. Since anger is said to manifest in our body as cancer, as a medical card this can indicate the presence of cancer.

QUEEN OF SWORDS: Air sign female (Aquarius, Gemini, Libra). Healer. Nurse, Energy worker. Reiki. Chiropractor. Female doctor. Teacher. A female soldier. Confident and strong woman. She has known pain and loss and become stronger from it. She offers healing to others. Any place that you go for healing. A clinic. A hospital. A spa. For pet readings, a veterinarian.

QUEEN OF SWORDS (Reversed): Unable to move forward past (his or her) own personal pain. Feelings are hurt. Feeling insulted. Wallowing in past injustices. Unwilling to forgive or forget. Bitterness. Controlling. Mistrust of others. Cold-hearted. Cruel. Hurtful. Sharp-tongued. Mean spirited. A single woman. Divorced or widowed woman.

KING OF SWORDS: Air sign male (Aquarius, Libra, Gemini). A soldier. A military leader. Serious and analytical (male or female). Strong-willed. Intelligent and independent. Perceptive. Someone involved in mental work. Researcher. Attorney. Lawyer. Counselor. Professor. Troubleshooter. He carries a tool or weapon in his profession. Surgeon. This card will usually be a real person rather than a situation.

KING OF SWORDS (Reversed): Terrorist. Neurotic. Grumpy. Grouch. Overbearing. Uses words to wound. Cruel. Cynical. Mocking. Fixed in his or her opinions. Difficult to deal with. Intense. Cold-hearted. Can be a domineering older woman. The military enemy. Could have a weapon and mean they are armed and dangerous. These negative qualities can represent male or female.

Cups

ACE OF CUPS: True love. Compassion. Passion for something. Being loved up on. Altruism. Sincerity. In good faith. Dedicated and loyal. Pregnancy (beating heart in a womb). Fertility. Birth of a child. Abundance (cup runneth over). Cups are the symbol of water, emotions, womb, feminine intuition, unconscious mind, being receptive (a vessel).

ACE OF CUPS (Reversed): Missing their loved one. Lost their love. Love spurned (rejected). Feeling empty and alone. Disappointment in love. Withholding their love. They are not in love. Never felt loved. Feeling unwanted or unloved. Lacking passion or desire for a thing, a person, or for sex. An unwanted pregnancy. Medical: Dehydration or fluid overload. Congestive heart failure.

2 OF CUPS: In agreement. Partnership. Relationship. Friendship. Best friends. Engaged. Merger. Mutual. Cooperation. Collaboration. Mentoring. Reciprocal. Reconciliation. Making arrangements. Sharing. Being supportive. Conception. Twins. Cell phone. Satellite. The number 2.

2 OF CUPS (Reversed): Broken friendships or relationships. Breaking or not honoring the agreement. Not making an agreement. Non reconciliation. Does not approve. Not cooperating. Rejects the proposal. A big quarrel. A falling out. Problem with the mentorship. Medically: Problem with the kidneys (renal).

3 OF CUPS: Celebration. Holiday. Party. Dancing. Socializing. A gathering. A meeting. Ceremony. Merriment. Many people involved. A women's group or women's club. Women in general. Family reunion, or gathering. Any occasion where people are together. Food or drink. Alcohol is involved. The kitchen. A club or restaurant. Works with food: waitress, cook, or chef.

3 OF CUPS (Reversed): Celebration turned to disappointment. An unhappy occasion, such as a funeral. A meeting goes bad. Wants to party all the time. Problem with food and drink such as contamination, bacteria, toxicity, poisoning. Partaking in too much food or alcohol. Gluttony. Fasting. Having no food. Hungry. Starving. Famine. Medically: Diabetic. Alcoholic. Food allergies. Malnutrition. Anorexia. Bulimia.

4 OF CUPS: Discontented. Not satisfied. Disappointed. Disinterested. Withdrawal. Melancholy. Apathy. Unmotivated. Laziness. Couldn't care less. Unfulfilled. Stubborn. Hard-headed. Not knowing what one wants. Brooding. Moody. Pessimistic. Melancholy. Despondent. A negative person. A 'downer". A naysayer. No fun to be around. Being a "wet blanket". Lacks enthusiasm or passion. Lacks attention or focus. Their glass is always half empty. Rejecting help offered.

4 OF CUPS (Reversed): Motivated. Determined. Made up their mind. Uncompromising. Unwavering. Focused. Deliberate. Conviction in opinion or action. Unshakable. Bring on hyper-alert. Noticing everything.

5 OF CUPS: Grief, loss, and despair. Sorrow. Regrets. Mourning. Grieving. Misery. Great disappointment. Disillusioned. Medically: Blood loss. Anemia.

5 OF CUPS (Reversed): Recovering emotionally from grief and loss. There are no regrets. They are not grieving. The reason for feeling sorrow is over with. Starting anew. A clean slate. Recovering what you lost.

6 OF CUPS: Children. Kids. Brothers and sisters. Cousins. Nieces and nephews. A group of kids. A place where there are lots of children; schools, colleges, daycare's. Pets that are loved and treated as children. Their childhood. The root of a situation is from their childhood. They know this person from their childhood.

6 OF CUP (Reversed): Problem with the children. Juvenile delinquents. Gang member. A gang of kids. A run away. Trouble with your siblings. They lost a child to a death or in a custody battle. A sickly child. Homeless children. They are childless. Could indicate that they do not like the children, or don't like kids, period! A troubled and unhappy childhood. Abused or neglected children.

7 OF CUPS: Imagination. Wondering. Daydreaming. Fantasy. Infatuation. Illusion. Delusional. Unrealistic. It's all in their head. Irrational. Visualizing. Having visions. A dream. Many choices. A speculation. Muddled. Faking it. It's fake. Faux. A facsimile. Counterfeit. Costume. Make believe. A play. Actresses and Actors. Represents all entertainment, arts and crafting. Pictures. Paintings. A painter. Artist. Photographer. Musician. Decorator. Auditory or visual hallucinations. A misunderstanding. Read literally: smoke, dust, fog, fumes, odors, heavy smoker, ash (same for reversed). This card repeatedly came up for the Russian fires of July/August 2010.

7 OF CUPS (Reversed): Misunderstanding. Misconceptions. Misinterpreting. Twisting reality to fit one's needs. Unable to discern between reality and illusion. Imagination running wild. Living in a fantasy world. Not what it appears to be. An illusion. Deceptive appearance. A disguise or it is disguised. Mistaken identity. False or stolen identity. Identity crisis. Bad dreams. Nightmares. Heavy smoker. Something wrong with the air. Unable to breathe. Toxic air. Fumes. Foul odors. Dust. Pollution. Pollen. Smoke. Carbon monoxide. The upright and reversed definitions are about the same.

8 OF CUPS: Walking away from a relationship or something one invested time, emotion, and energy in. Leaving everything behind (physically, emotionally or metaphorically). Putting it behind you. Abandoning a plan or project. Turning their back. Getting smooth away with it. Change of plans. Going in a new direction. Breaking new ground. Innovation. Exploring the unknown. Pioneering. Hiking. Emigrants (legal or illegal). Refugees. Evacuating. This card repeatedly came up for the mass evacuations of hurricane Katrina.

8 OF CUPS (Reversed): Not walking away. Deciding to stay. Staying even if it is hopeless and pointless, or no longer rewarding or beneficial. They are refusing to leave when you've asked them to go. Or, they won't go where you are wanting them to go. Wandering around lost. Having Alzheimer's.

9 OF CUPS: Happy. Friendly. Satisfaction. Joy. Fulfilled. Contentment. Achievement. Feeling of abundance. You get what you wanted. Happy with the outcome. Pleasant person. Extravagant or comfortable lifestyle. Generosity. A jolly, funny person. A comedian. Good intentions. Laughing. Many times this card will be upright and represent being depressed; especially if it appears in the "thinking" position. Can indicate manic depressive or a split personality (even if upright).

9 OF CUPS (Reversed): Unhappy. Depressed. A person who is never satisfied and who is difficult or impossible to please. Emotionally unstable. Mood swings. Manic depressive. You will not get what you wished for. Their intentions are unfriendly. Does not like them. An unpleasant personality.

10 OF CUPS: Happy family. A family united in love and joy. A devoted family. Focus is on family and is important to them. An adopted family. A family reunion. Family increases. Starting a family. Can be any group that makes you feel loved or treated as part of the family. A large, extended family. Feeling fulfilled.

10 OF CUPS (Reversed): Problems with the family. Family members are quarreling. Disconnected from family. Ostracized from or kicked out of the family. Broken home due to divorce or death. Family has grown apart. They do not have a family. An orphan. Grew up in foster care. Feeling their family is not complete. Lost an important family member. Missing their family. Homesick.

PAGE OF CUPS: A child. A young person with artistic, intuitive and psychic abilities. The child is intelligent, gifted, and creative. A much beloved child. A favorite child. A good student. A child who brings joy. Any free spirited person no matter the age. Young at heart. Can represent a female child if question is of gender.

PAGE OF CUPS (Reversed): There is a problem with this child. Physically or mentally handicapped. Mental retardation. Mongoloid. Mentally incompetent. Crippled. An emotionally disturbed child. A worrisome child. The word 'disabled' in relation to person or to an object. The word 'unable'. Working with the disabled. A self-centered, childish person of any age.

KNIGHT OF CUPS: Romance. The arrival of a suitor. Wooing or being wooed. Declaration of love. Love offering. Dating. A marriage proposal. Offering or receiving a proposal or proposition. A good opportunity. In good faith. Benefiting. Prospecting. Having good potential. Someone who travels over the ocean and waters. A seafaring person. Flooding issues.

KNIGHT OF CUPS (Reversed): Cheating. Infidelity. An affair. Unfaithful lover. Taking their love elsewhere. Relationship based on deceit and lies. The romance is off. This person does not really care about you and will never make a commitment. An unrequited, unreturned love interest. Being suspicious of unfaithfulness, whether true or unfounded. To determine if they are truly cheating look for court cards that represent other people or the 7 of swords (be careful telling a seeker their love is cheating on them). No prospects, no offers, no opportunities. Medically: Edema, fluid overload. Pleurisy.

QUEEN OF CUPS: A water sign woman (Pisces, Scorpio, Cancer). Mother. Wife. A mother figure (any female relative). An affectionate woman. A beautiful woman. She is highly creative and artistic. She has psychic ability and insight. One's appearance. Beauty. Beautician. Cosmetics. The physical appearance of a thing or object. A light haired or light skinned woman.

QUEEN OF CUPS (Reversed): Troubles with their mother, wife, female relative, ex-wife or ex-girlfriend. A bad mother. No mothering skills. An argumentative wife. A cheating wife. A dishonest, untrustworthy woman. A gossiping woman. Being gossiped about. Being betrayed by a woman. The 'other' woman. They don't find her pretty or she feels unattractive for some reason. An item that is not in good cosmetic condition. Skin or other 'cosmetic' problems. Problem with one's appearance. Medically: Cosmetic issues. Acne. Boils. Scars. Skin cancer. Disfigured.

KING OF CUPS: Husband. Father. A father figure. Father in law. A water sign man (Pisces, Cancer, Scorpio). Doctor. A light haired or light skinned male. An emotional, sensitive, or tender-hearted male. Mentoring male who is supportive. The big-brother type.

KING OF CUPS (Reversed): Problem with husband or father. An ex-husband. Estranged husband. Husband has left the wife. Personality or character flaws in a man. A dishonest and untrustworthy male. Emotional betrayal. A rejection or neglect issue with their father, husband, or the father of the children. Either the seeker is the one being denied or rejected by this male figure, or they are doing the rejecting. A person who says one thing and does another. Makes promises but doesn't follow through.

Wands

ACE OF WANDS: Creation. Life. Birth. Fertility. Pregnant. Creativity. Brilliant or profitable idea. Inspired. Inventions. Lucrative business endeavors. Physical chemistry. Lots of Charisma. Thrilling. Exciting. They are alive. Dynamic. Attraction. Hormones. Enzymes. Electricity. Energy. Magnetic. Carries a charge. Nuclear power. Radiation. Laser. Multi media. Video. Biological or chemical organisms. DNA. Sperm. Ova. Genetics.

ACE OF WANDS (Reversed): We are biological, chemical and electrical organisms. Our bodies are run by hormones, chemicals, neurotransmitters. Problems with these processes are too numerous to list. Provided are just a few. Genetic problem or birth defects. Dead versus alive. Infertility. Neurological disorders. Seizures. Parkinson's. Fibromyalgia. Chronic fatigue. Multiple Sclerosis. Chemical imbalances in the brain. Manic Depressive. Depression. Hormone problems. PMS. Inflammatory processes. Sprains. Broken bone. Bone marrow problems (leukemia, neutropenia). Allergic reactions (anaphylaxis), immuno-suppressed. Bacteria & viruses (flu, SARS, small pox, hepatitis, herpes, molds, fungus, anthrax, Ebola, HIV). Bio-chemical organism (natural or man-made). Radiation or chemotherapy. Antibiotics (against life). Electrical problems. Radioactive. Shocked or electrocuted. Fire. Explosion. Fireworks. Hot. Burn. Gun-shot or bullet.

2 OF WANDS: Self-esteem and confidence. Having goals. Strong, healthy ego. A capable person who is ready to move forward in life and is surveying their prospects. Prospects look good. They are ambitious and building upon past successes. Having a good outlook on life. The "world is their oyster". They can pursue anything they please. Someone or something is good for their ego and self-esteem. Anticipation. Watching and waiting for something. Awaiting a response from someone.

2 OF WANDS (Reversed): Poor self-esteem and lack of confidence. They have no goals. They have no idea what they want to do with their life. No successes to build upon. Not advancing or progressing. Not being assertive. Not a go-getter. Having insecurities. Under-estimating ones abilities. Feeling incapable. Settling for less. The prospects are poor. Someone or something is damaging their ego and self-esteem. Sudden loss of self-confidence due to a precipitating event. An issue of ego (too much or too little).

3 OF WANDS: Business success. Successful merchant. Business owner. Entrepreneur. Networking. Expanding. New prospects or business relations. Importing & exporting. Wealth through international exchange. Looking to join up with (such as marines, or armed forces). Oil rich countries (oil=liquid gold). Off shore oil drilling (came up for British Petroleum spill). Fracking.

3 OF WANDS (Reversed): Business problems. Business is slowed. Poor prospects. Going out of business, willingly or unwillingly. The business is down or has failed. Warning that it is not a good business venture. The company is not sound. Trouble with oil countries or oil companies.

4 OF WANDS: Marriage. A wedding. Romance. Building a life together as a couple. Living together as if married. Establishing a firm foundation in any relationship, including friendships. Providing a solid foundation for another, including children. Sharing your life with another (of any age or relation). Can refer to the foundation or structure of a home or building. Being on solid ground with an issue or person.

4 OF WANDS (Reversed): A relationship (legally married or not) that is over or is not working. Wanting out of the marriage. Divorced. One party refuses to marry the other. Never been married. An unfaithful marriage. Not having a strong foundation to the endeavor or relationship; nothing to build upon. Problems with the foundation, roof, or structure when asking about a house or building. For example, this card with the 5 of pentacles would indicate structural problems because the foundation is "sick" or "injured".

5 OF WANDS: Mental anxiety. Mental conflicts. Obstacles. Strife. Struggle. Competition. Rivalry. Indecision. Excessive mental activity. Trying to mentally solve a problem. Over thinking. Worrying. General anxiety disorder. Post-traumatic stress disorder.

5 OF WANDS (Reversed): Not worrying anymore. They aren't worried about it. Not giving any thought to it.

6 OF WANDS: Honor and appreciation. Admiration. Public acclamation. Public vindication. Honored. Someone famous. Celebrity. A public figure. Admired and well respected. Being well received. A returning hero. Recognized in their field. Reaching goals. A good reputation. Triumph. Victory.

6 OF WANDS (Reversed): Not being, or just not feeling appreciated. Not being acknowledged. Being, or just feeling disrespected and dishonored. A plan or action did not succeed. Defamation of character. Having a bad reputation. Receiving a negative referral or reference. Their background check is bad.

7 OF WANDS: Success. Winning. Overcoming obstacles. Coming out on top. Holding one's ground. Taking a stand. Having the upper hand or advantage. Facing the opposition. Accepting the challenge. You will succeed.

7 OF WANDS (Reversed): Unsuccessful. Failing. Won't win. Will not challenge. They quit or want to quit. Gave up. Surrendering. Easily influenced or easily swayed. Being over ruled or outnumbered. Obstacles are too great and cannot be overcome. Insurmountable. This is a losing battle.

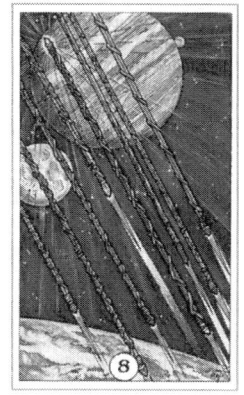

8 OF WANDS: Advancement. Expanding. Prospering. Growth happening. Job promotion. Rapid action or motion. Movement. Activity. Taking action. Projectile. Missiles. Sudden attack. Speeding. Fast. Quickly. Done hastily. Going far (physically or metaphorically). Indicates time. Gaining more time. A long time. A timeline. Spanning several generations. Outer space. Planets. Comets. Meteorites. Observatory. Astronomy. Astrology. Space program. The space shuttle.

8 OF WANDS (Reversed): No advancement happening. Delays and stagnation. Losing ground. Going backwards. Overdue. On hold. Boredom. Period of inaction. Not happening fast enough. Too slow. Too fast. Lack of time. Not the right time to take action. Bad timing. Speed causes a problem. Physical exhaustion. Burnout. Stimulants. Amphetamines. Caffeine.

9 OF WANDS: On the defensive. Taking a stand. Defending oneself or another. Willing to do battle. Won't back down. Determined. Prepared to fight. Guarding. Being on guard. Security guard. Anticipating struggles. Encountering obstacles. Facing difficulties. Maintaining their position. Defiance. A struggle. A martial artist (Karate). Skilled in art of self-defense. Survivalist. Prepper.

9 OF WANDS (Reversed): They quit, gave up. Losing the battle. Cut your losses and get out. Whatever it was, it is over. Releasing the need to struggle. Refusing to face the challenge. Doesn't like confrontation. Won't confront them. Unequipped. Does not possess the skill to face the challenge. Easily over-whelmed by obstacles. Unable to defend one's position. Defenseless. No backbone. Lacks willpower and determination.

10 OF WANDS: A hard worker. Doing their duty. All work, no play. Taking on the responsibility. Taking on more than you can handle. Over-worked. Keeping their nose to the grindstone. Working on their feet or carrying heavy loads. Carrying the guilt (weight on their shoulders). They are a carrier, courier, or deliver things. Carried on their person. Walking, hiking, jogging. Medical: Hip, back or knee problems making it difficult to walk.

10 OF WANDS (Reversed): Burden lifted. Refusing to support themselves. Being dependent on others. Letting others carry their load. Laziness. Being irresponsible. Medically: Difficulty walking. Walking stooped over. Hunch back. Walks with a limp. Back, hip or knee problems. Uses walker, cane, or special shoes. Osteoarthritis. Weight issues (too heavy or too thin).

PAGE OF WANDS: Giving or receiving a message. Invitation. Speaking. Calling. Talking. Yelling. Talking about it or hearing about it. Broadcasting it. Sounding an alarm. Making a noise of any kind. Marriage proposal. All forms of communication and media. All jobs that involve communication. Electronics. Video. Multimedia. Computers. Internet. Twitter. Skype. Youtube. Email. Texting. Faxing. Making a purchase. Buying. Selling. Public speaker. Seminar. Publishing. Electronic transfer of data. Reporters. Newspapers. Radio. Commercials. Marketing. Advertisement. Stock market. Broadcasting. Our communication senses (seeing, hearing, smelling, speaking).

PAGE OF WANDS (Reversed): Communication problems. Did not like what was communicated. Saying the wrong thing. An information problem or breakdown, whether in delivery or understanding. They cannot or will not communicate with you. Won't answer the phone, email, or texts. Having a problem with the language. Unable to use the equipment, or a problem with the equipment. Problems with multimedia, computers, the internet, the stock market, publishing, or advertisements. Problem with a purchase. Problems with buying or selling. All the reverse of the upright position. Medically: trouble hearing, seeing, or speaking. Laryngitis. Deafness. Mute. Aphasia.

KNIGHT OF WANDS: Traveling. Taking a trip. Moving. Changing residence. Taking action. Motivation. Quick, energetic, enthusiastic, or urgent action. Enthusiasm for taking an action. Traveling or driving as a career. Transportation. Truck or taxi driver. A moving company. Tow trucks. Delivery trucks. UPS. Being taken to jail (which is a change of residence or forced action). Read literally, horses or large animals. Having a muscular build.

KNIGHT OF WANDS (Reversed): Forced to change their residence. Thrown out of the house. Eviction. Forced to move where they don't want to move, including going to jail. Wishing they could move. Having to move out of necessity. Unable to take action. Slow to action, or not taking action. Forced into taking action. A trip is delayed or canceled. Problem with horses or large animals. Medically: muscular or neuromuscular disorders. Multiple sclerosis. Tremors. Parkinson's. Fibromyalgia. Gillian Barre. Muscular Dystrophy. Myasthenia Gravis. Muscle cramps.

QUEEN OF WANDS: Fire sign female (Aries, Leo, Sagittarius). A woman with stage presence. A speaker. A singer. Socially prominent. Actress. Performer. A 'social light'. Flair for drama. Likes being the center of attention and 'center-stage'. She is energetic, passionate, action oriented. A woman of any sign who has outgoing and energetic qualities. Blond or red haired woman.

QUEEN OF WANDS (Reversed): Socially withdrawn. Extremely shy. Anti-social. Isolated from others. Having an inhibited and reserved personality. They refuse to talk to someone, or someone is not talking to them. An alternative interpretation could be that this woman is jealous or vengeful. This person could be of any sign and have these positive or negative qualities.

KING OF WANDS: Fire sign male (Aries, Leo, Sagittarius). An assertive, energetic, enthusiastic, passionate male. Charismatic. Salesman. Entertainer. Musician. Stage or public personality. Famous and well known. Very sociable and enjoys being the center of attention. A blond or red haired man. American Indian. A gay male.

KING OF WANDS (Reversed): A man with all the negative characteristics of the upright King of Wands. Loud and obnoxious. Obstinate behavior. Disgusting and obscene. Hostile. Belligerent. Combative. An assaulter. A man who is clinging to a female in a jealous fashion. An ex husband or ex boyfriend.

Pentacles

ACE OF PENTACLES: Financial success and security. A successful business venture. Large investment. Those who handle a lot of money. A stock or bond. Capital gains. Startup capital. Receiving a sum of money. Something is expensive. Huge expenses. The physical, manifested realm. The earth. The physical body. Can represent anything physical, such as equipment.

ACE OF PENTACLES (Reversed): Great loss of money. Financial ruin. Bankruptcy. Large amount of money spent. A large down payment. Large debt or payment owed. Maxed out the credit cards. Heavy loss in the stock market. Poverty. Could just represent fears about being broke if in the thinking position. The soul is earthbound (in questions about a departed loved one). Broken equipment. Equipment failure. A thing or person being in poor physical condition. Physical assault and battery.

2 OF PENTACLES: Balanced. Stable. Capable. Multitasking. Good technique. Performing well under pressure. A 'balancing act'. Weighing a dilemma. Deliberating on the pros and cons of a matter, or two equally attractive prospects in order to make a choice. Prospecting. Forming an opinion. Things are "still up in the air". Two of a thing. An exchange or transfer. Mixing or combining things. Switching of two things. It is cyclic. A thing spinning. Tornado. El' Nino. Hurricane. A cable or phone company. Wiring or transferring money. Cables or wires. Wheels. Medically: the legs, feet and ankles. Having a fall. Hurting a leg, foot, or ankle (same for reversed card). This card kept coming up for hurricane Katrina (plus 8 cups for evacuations).

2 OF PENTACLES (Reversed): Falling. Tripping. Breaking, spraining, or hurting a leg, foot, or ankle. Problems with leg or foot area. Needing shoes, special shoes or wheel chair. Thrown off balance. Vertigo. Loss of equilibrium. Unable to juggle demands. Overwhelmed. Not able to formulate an opinion or make a choice. Two items are unequal, not the same in some way. Not having the same value as the other. It's a 'bait and switch'. Too

much of one thing compared to another. A thing out of balance. Problems with phone, cable company, or electrical wiring. Problem wiring money.

3 OF PENTACLES: A job. Getting a new job. An increase in rank, duty, prestige and earnings. A master craftsman. Skilled in a profession or trade. A trained craft. Having marketable skills. Intricate detailed work. Sculpting. Chiseling. Carving. Building something. Indicates it is manmade. Creating something of enduring and lasting beauty. Working on something, like a project.

3 OF PENTACLES (Reversed): Lost their job. Laid off. No pleasure in their work, or not being able to work. Stuck in a job they don't like. No marketable skills. Not skilled at their current job. Unskilled labor. Poor workmanship. They have no job. Resigning. They don't want to work. Work alcoholic versus lazy. Problems with a project.

4 OF PENTACLES: Possessive. Greedy. Selfish. Envy. Clinging. Won't share. Mistrustful. Afraid someone is going to take it away. Unable to let go of a thing tangible or intangible. They want it back. Hanging on in a stubborn way. They, like, really - really want it. Hoarding. Squirreling it away. In their possession. Keeping it private. Being protective. Tucking something or <u>someone</u> away for safe-keeping. Hidden from prying eyes. protecting one's privacy. Keeping it private. Securing it. A safe. Guarding what they have. Wants others to stay away. Hiding out. A hideout. A storm shelter.

4 OF PENTACLES (Reversed): Releasing. Letting it go. Forgiving and forgetting. Forgiveness. The message is to let it go (physically or metaphorically). They do not hold it as being dear to them. There are no safeguards or protections being provided or awarded to it. A thing or person is not being kept safe. Medical: problem in arms, wrists, or hands. Arthritis.

5 OF PENTACLES: Illness. Injury. Disease. Sick. Being in poor health. Declining health. Aging. Physical deterioration. Poverty. Being poor. Impoverished. Having a feeling of being poor. Feeling or being destitute. Suffering. Hardships. Outcast. Feeling rejected. Mistreated. Suffering violence. Physical abuse. Neglected. Abandoned. Beggar. Homeless. Medical: all illnesses or injury. Amputations.

5 OF PENTACLES (Reversed): Health restored. Reversal of poverty. Health issue correctable or in the process of correcting. Illness in remission. Healing taking place. They will recover. Works with the handicapped, injured, or abused (up right or reversed).

6 OF PENTACLES: Financial stability. Paying all the bills, debts and creditors. Making ends meet with something left over. They owe a lot of people. Sharing. Charity. Donating. Helping the less fortunate in times of need. Giving or receiving assistance; usually involves financial aid given but can be any help rendered. Humanitarian aid. On financial aid.

6 OF PENTACLES (Reversed): Not making ends meet. Unable to pay all the bills. Too many bills and creditors. Financially unstable. Over drawn. Over-extended. Bounced checks. Unable to support themselves. Not receiving the assistance they needed or expected. Wanting to help but not able to. No giving or receiving is going on.

7 OF PENTACLES: Work. Getting a new job. Menial or manual labor. Handyman. Farmer. Gardener. Gardening. Landscaping. Plants. Construction worker. Loves the outdoors. Woodsman. A hunter. Time to reap the rewards from their labor. A plan that comes to fruition. Harvest time. Satisfaction from a job well done. This card is interchangeable with 3 of pentacles for job or work. The message, "In due time". Could be read as a period of 7 months (or sometime within the next 7 months).

7 OF PENTACLES (Reversed): Lost or quit the job. Looking for work. Don't like or want the job. Unable to reap the harvest of their hard work. Long laid plans are dashed. There is no future potential in the project. Disappointment or failure in some enterprise.

8 OF PENTACLES: Training. Studying. School. Classroom. Reading. Writing. Signature. Autograph. Reports. Paper work. Books. Documents. Notarized. Clerical. Contract. Records. Journal. Diary. Email. Letter. A writer. A teacher. A student. Studious child. Learning a new skill or knowledge. Learning the tools of the trade. Apprenticeship. Craftsmanship. Working with wood, cabinetmaking, wood carvings. Assembling. Concentrating on the work at hand. Planning. They planned it.

8 OF PENTACLES (Reversed): Untrained. Uneducated. Illiterate. Drop-out. Failing. Skipped school. Reading or learning disability. Lied about their training or education. Didn't do their homework. Didn't do their due diligence. Didn't read it. Problem with a document or contract. Undocumented illegal immigrant. Dread signing papers (divorce, etc.').

9 OF PENTACLES: Affluent. Wealthy. Financially secure. Above average income. Feeling secure and self-confident. Material comforts. Pampered, sheltered life. Well dressed. Elegance. One's personal and material possessions. Unscathed by turmoil's affecting others. Luxury items (jewelry, cloths, furniture). Actual garden or flowers. Outdoors. Outside. Land. Acreage. A secured environment, boundary, area, or compound. FEMA camps. A shelter. A "safe house" or safe haven.

9 OF PENTACLES (Reversed): Loss of wealth or personal property. Loss of financial independence, possibly having to rely on another for financial support. Bad financial planning. Having lost 'the farm'. Bankruptcy. Feelings of insecurity or a lack of confidence. This is not a safe or secure environment. Border or compound is not secure.

10 OF PENTACLES: Home. House. Apartment. Office. Hotel room. A room. Any building. In the house. Homemaker. Focus is on home and family. Time off to stay home. Home bound. A peaceful and tranquil home and family life. Planning to purchase a home. Renovations or home improvements. In the business of home construction, home repairs, real estate, or investor.

10 OF PENTACLES (Reversed): Disruptive or unhappy home life. Too many people in the house. Evicted or thrown out. Having no place to live. Lost the house. Foreclosure. Afraid to leave the house (agoraphobia). Homebound. Grounded. Structural problems (roof leaks, foundation cracked, appliances broke). Living in the projects. Fights over who gets the house. You don't get the house.

PAGE OF PENTACLES: Payments, dues, and fees. Gifts. Child support. Money or gifts to a child. An allowance. Paying for school, classes, private school or college. A grant or scholarship. A bonus check. Sharing. An item of value. Payments made in installments (on layaway). Payback is now due. Making restitution. The 8 rays can indicate portions, parts or portions of a whole, or fractions of a whole or indicate blocks of time. 6 months. Ethnic child. A non-biological child.

PAGE OF PENTACLES (Reversed): Not sharing or giving a portion. Not giving a gift. No money for school supplies or education. No grants, loans, or scholarship. No money to the kids. Unable to support the child's expenses. No child support. Not receiving a gift. Lost money (purse, wallet, credit card, etc.'). Nonpayment (credit cards, rent, fees). Unable to buy or purchase an item. The step-child. Rejects the child. Can mean, "because it is not their child." A lazy, non-productive child. Parts of a whole but not the whole. Parts missing. Partially. Part time.

KNIGHT OF PENTACLES: Getting a bank loan. Getting credit cards. Getting checks or other payments. Getting a nice sum of money. Someone of a reliable nature who helps them in any way. Making good money. Receiving or giving personal or financial assistance to others.

KNIGHT OF PENTACLES (Reversed): Not getting the loan. Not getting the financial help they need. They do not support you. Problems with money. An unreliable person, probably uninterested in employment. They are not financially dependable. Lost significant amount of money. Bad credit reports. Lost the credit card or lost the checks.

QUEEN OF PENTACLES: Earth-sign woman (Virgo, Capricorn, Taurus). Handles money or loans. Works for a bank or in a loan department. Good business practices. Efficient and dependable woman. A practical and 'down to earth' woman; not necessarily an earth sign. An ethnic woman with dark hair and skin. Things that are "earthy," meaning dirt, fruits and vegetables.

** This card consistently came up for the smoldering and burning peat-moss of the Russian fires in July 2010. Pentacles are the physical realm and Queen of Pentacles is "earth-woman" and hence represents products of 'mother-earth'. It is interesting that the nickname for Russia is the 'Mother-Land'. Other cards were 7 Cups + 8 Cups for smoke and evacuations.

QUEEN OF PENTACLES (Reversed): Woman of reduced means. She is broke. Being impractical in business. A woman financially dependent on others. Handles money poorly. She might manage money appropriately but be in a temporary position where money is tight.

KING OF PENTACLES: Earth sign male (Virgo, Capricorn, Taurus). Wealthy. A rich man or woman. Old money. Financially established person. A large savings (nest egg). Comfortable retirement. 401k's. Retirement funds. A corporate head who manages the money. Financial institutions. Banks. Stock markets. Bank rolling a project. A reliable man that you can financially count on.

KING OF PENTACLES (Reversed): A huge financial loss. Loss of savings or retirement money. Keep an eye on your accounts and take precautions. No financial means or backing. Heavily in debt. Financial stress. A financial institution that is in trouble. Shady business practices. Dishonest businessman. He will take you for your money. Scrutinize all business contracts and negotiations. Squanders the money away. Medically: Liver problems (the liver is the master organ).

Two Card combinations

Major

Fool + 8 Cups: Starting a new adventure. Wandering into unfamiliar territory, either physically or metaphorically. They don't know where they are going, they are just going.

Fool + 2 Swords: Making a decision while lacking the experience. Crossroads that brings new beginnings. Wasn't aware that a decision or crossroads or choice was ahead.

Fool + Judgement: They are young and healthy. Item is brand new or like brand new and in good working order. Starting all over anew.

Fool (rev) + 8 Pentacles: A learning disability. School for the mentally or physically handicapped. Classes for the slow learner. Remedial reading. Writing stupid or foolish things.

Magician + 2 Cups: Mentoring with or collaborating with someone who is well skilled in their craft. Two highly skilled individuals form a partnership.

Magician + 9 Wands: Rugged or bearded security guard, body guard, or life guard. Defending or guarding this rugged, bearded man. Skilled in the art of self-defense.

Magician + 10 Pentacles: A skilled builder, architect, or handyman. The house or building has been well constructed.

Magician (rev) + 7 Pentacles (rev): Having no marketable job skills. Problems with their job due to poor performance.

High Priestess + Justice: Top secret or confidential legal information. A deposition or court order to gain classified information or secrets. Making a legal decision based upon right information. A lie-detector test.

High Priestess + 7 Wands: They have some inside information that is going to give them the upper hand, and the success and victory they needed.

High Priestess + Page Wands: Broadcasting inside or private information. Making secret information known. This is what a whistle-blower would look like. An example would be Edward Snowden and the NSA.

High Priestess (rev) + 2 Cups (rev): Too introverted and shy to form the relationship or friendship. Or, information that was exposed or revealed broke the deal or friendship.

Empress + 5 Wands: Worried about a pregnancy or worried if they can even get pregnant. Worried about one's mother, an elder, or worried about a babysitter or caregiver situation.

Empress + Ace Wands: Definitely pregnant. The pregnancy will be a live birth. The baby and/or mother will survive. No birth defects indicated because Ace of Wands is upright. You can check for birth defects by deliberately reversing the Ace of Wands (or page cups) and see if you still get it.

Empress + King Cups: A gynecologist or baby doctor. The baby's biological daddy. This man is associated with a pregnant woman in some way. A man and his elder mother, or a husband and his pregnant wife.

Empress (rev) + 6 swords (rev): They don't get to go on the trip because they can't get a babysitter or because there isn't anyone to care for their elderly parent or other elderly relative.

Emperor + Queen Wands: Woman in a position of authority and power. The boss or owner is a woman. This leader (president/dictator) has a woman in his presence who is either a fire-sign or has red hair. Combination came up for Palestinian president, Arafat, whose wife was a strawberry blond.

Emperor + 9 Wands: Standing your ground in the face of authority. Or, a power person comes to their defense. Defending someone else against authority. Defending a person who is in a position of authority. Or, a powerful person and their body guard.

Emperor + 8 Swords: Being confined or restricted by an official. A restraining order. A cease and desist order. Possibly a powerful figure under house arrest. They have the authority or power but are being kept from taking action on it.

Emperor (rev) + Devil: Stuck in a negative, toxic relationship with a domineering and controlling person. Or, drugs are causing this person to behave in an obnoxious way.

Hierophant + Page Wands: A religious radio or television broadcast. Promoting religion through speech, commercials, song, or other medium. A religious personality on stage. Speaking a foreign language. Church bells, or call to prayer as is done in Islam. Announcing they are gay.

Hierophant + 8 Pentacles (rev): An undocumented illegal alien. Or, a foreigner is having other issues with their documents or paperwork (passport issues?). Church has problems with Sunday school or bibles.

Hierophant + 6 Pentacles: Tithing or giving to the church or other traditional institution to help the less fortunate. Giving to charity or making religiously motivated donations. Or, a religious based institution offers them financial support (clothes, electric, food).

Hierophant (rev) + Queen Swords (rev): Feeling betrayed and hurt by their church or church members. Hurt caused by prejudices such as racism, because they are a foreigner, or because they are gay.

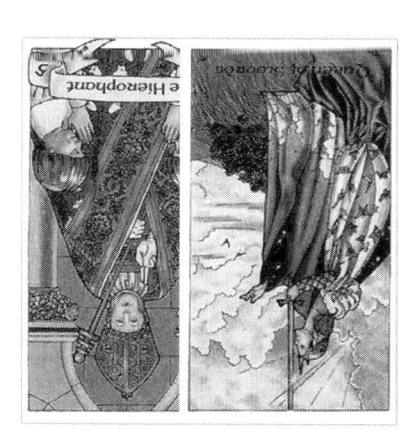

Lovers + 2 Wands: Their love interest has boosted their ego and self-esteem. Or, they are waiting, watching for, or anticipating the arrival of their lover or partner.

Lovers + 5 Pentacles: Their partner is sick or injured. Any illness or infection that is sexually or otherwise contagious from one person to another (not necessarily sexually transmitted). Their partner is physically abusive. Sexual abuse is happening.

Lovers + 9 Cups: They are very happy about the relationship (theirs or someone else's). A very happy or generous couple.

Lovers (rev) + 3 Swords: Definite end to this relationship. A divorce. Devastated and heartbroken over the loss of their partner. Their partner could have been killed. End of relationship could also be due to infidelity or cheating because the lovers card is reversed.

Chariot + Devil: Driving under the influence of alcohol or drugs. Transporting drugs. A drug runner. Obsessing about the vehicle or about getting a vehicle. Toxic fumes from the vehicle. The oil is dirty or contaminated.

Chariot + 7 Swords: Car is stolen. A car thief. Being spied on or followed by someone in a car. Being lied to or deceived about a vehicle. A crooked car dealer or crooked mechanic. Vehicle was sabotaged. Car towed (sneaky act).

Chariot + Knight of Swords: Pulled over by the police. Getting a ticket. A rescue vehicle of any type; ambulance, fire truck, boat. Angry about a vehicle. (Even though Knight of Swords isn't reversed, can still take its reversed position for anger).

Chariot (rev) + Ace Pentacles (rev): Vehicle is not structurally sound (physical or mechanical problems). Repossession of vehicle due to non-payment. Expensive repairs.

Strength + 3 Cups (rev): The pet doesn't like their food or they won't eat for some reason. Pet is diabetic. Person who is allergic to certain foods or drinks (because Strength card can represent allergies and of course reversed 3 of cups is problems with food or drink).

Strength + Queen Swords: A pet clinic or veterinarian. A person with calming and healing abilities. Their pet provides healing for them. A "therapy pet".

Strength + Hermit (rev): The animal is going blind. The animal is lost or can't find its way. A seeing-eye dog. The animal is old (rev Hermit). A search and rescue animal for someone or something that can't be found.

Strength (rev) + 5 pentacles: In a weakened condition due to illness or injury. Illness or diseases spread by animals. The animal is sick, injured, or is being abused or neglected. Fear about an illness. Hypochondriac.

Hermit + 7 Swords: Investigating or exposing a criminal record or criminal act. A criminal background check. Crime is caught on surveillance or it was videotaped, for example captured on camera phone.

Hermit + 2 Swords: Research, consulting, professional or expert advice or opinion went into making this decision. Or, this research caused them to make changes.

Hermit + 3 Cups: Looking for food or drink. Food or drink that is very old (outdated). Searching for a group of people. A research committee. A committee or group of people who investigate or search for a thing.

Hermit (rev) + 10 Pentacles: The house or building is dark and not lighted. There is no surveillance at the building. Can't find the house or building.

Wheel of Fortune + 3 Wands: Good fortune in business. Inherited the business. Investing the money in business overseas. Wealth made in oil.

Wheel of Fortune + 7 Cups: Daydreaming or fantasizing about an inheritance or winning the lottery, and imagining what they would do with the wealth.

Wheel of Fortune + Ace Wands: Fantastic creative invention that brings wealth or good fortune. Lucky to be alive. Feels fortunate or lucky to be pregnant.

Wheel of Fortune (rev) + 8 Wands (rev): Misfortune causes advances and progress to come to a halt.

Justice + Page of Pentacles: Court ordered payments of child support. Legal fees or dues. Insurance payments. Attorney fees. Court costs. Paying fines or tickets. Small claims court. Garnished wages.

Justice + 8 Swords: Judge or court sends them to jail. Prisoner appearing before the courts. A restraining order. Legally binding or obligated. Legal restrictions. Bail bondsman.

Justice + 8 Cups: The case gets dropped. They get to walk away from the legal situation. They are forced by the legal system to relinquish their claims, or they legally have to leave.

Justice (rev) + Death (rev): There seems to be no end in sight for this legal problem. A legal issue that has been on-going for a long time and seems to have stalemated and isn't budging.

Hanged man + 2 Pentacles: Situation is in limbo while things are being deliberated (the pros and cons). Or, head or neck injury due to a fall (even though 2 pents isn't reversed). It could even be that a life hangs in the balance and a debate is occurring on how to handle the situation.

Hanged man + Death: End of something that has been in limbo. Astral body of someone who is deceased; could just be "dropping in". Bite from something (spider, snake, scorpion) causes decay or death of tissue, not necessarily death of the individual unless with other negative cards.

Hanged man + 5 Cups: Grieving over someone so ill that their life "hangs by a thread" and could go either way. Stuck in a mode of grieving so that everything else has been put on hold (limbo). Blood loss from head or neck.

Hanged man (rev) + 3 Cups: Choking on food or swelling of throat due to food allergy. Negative aspects of "partying" behavior or alcohol addiction caused by the influence of an earthbound spirit. Could also be read that there are several spirits present.

Death + 9 Cups: We'll start with a positive combination for this card. There is someone on the other side, a deceased person, who is wishing you well and expressing that they are pleased with you. Or, the client is happy that something has ended.

Death + 10 Pentacles: There is a deceased person in the house. Home hospice where they want to die at home. A funeral home or morgue.

Death + 10 Wands: The end of something has led to hard work or them having to take on responsibility. Other cards in the layout or discussion with client will elaborate.

Death (rev) + 7 Swords: Chronic criminal activity; and they don't planning on quitting. This would be a habitual "career" criminal.

Temperance + 5 Wands: Putting a lot of mental activity or worry into making sure things run smoothly. It's also possible that despite things running smoothly, they constantly worry.

Temperance + 8 Wands: Things are running smoothly (like a well-oiled machine) so that much progress, advances, or promotions are being made. Angelic intervention brings advancement.

Temperance + 2 Swords: Changes made will be pulled off without a hitch because everything comes together for a smooth transition and with flow.

Temperance (rev) + 3 Pentacles (rev): There is a lot of stress going on at their job. They are experiencing job burnout. They might even quit their job because of the stress.

Devil + Page Swords (rev): Hyperactive or out of control child due to drugs, chemicals or environmental contaminants. Or, refers to medications prescribed for a child with behavioral issues. An adult with childish behavioral problems due to drugs.

Devil + Ace Swords (rev): A negative relationship or situation that includes hostility and aggression (rev swords). A hostile and dangerous situation due to drugs.

Devil + 10 Pentacles: Toxins in the home (mold, carbon monoxide, fumes, carpet, polyurethane counter tops, toxic pipes, lead paint, asbestos). A negative situation in the home. Drug use in the home or their room. A drug house (weed, crack, heroin, meth).

Devil (rev) + 10 Wands: Overcoming a drug addiction through hard work. Could be that their drug recovery is a constant struggle. Or, they are off drugs and being self-reliant.

Tower + 9 Pentacles: Being in a safe place (environment, enclosure) and away from the disaster. Going to locations of safety, like shelters, after a disaster.

Tower + Ace Wands (rev): Disaster related to explosion or fire. A major infectious outbreak. Devastated by a stroke, neurological issue, birth defect, etc.' The Tower causes the ace of wands to take on its multitude of negative definitions.

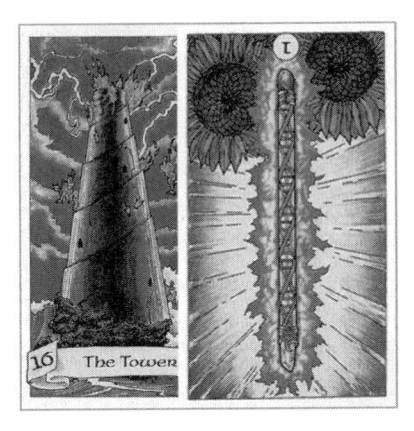

Tower + Chariot (rev): The vehicle (any form of transportation) ran into bad weather or met with some disaster. A vehicular accident. If buying a vehicle, consider that it has flood or other weather related damage.

Tower (rev) + Hermit: Exposing or investigating what could potentially have been a disaster. Disaster diverted because it had been revealed (shedding light on it) before it could happen.

Star + Knight of Cups: An opportunity or proposition being offered that allows them to realize their greatest aspirations, hopes and dreams.

Star + 8 Wands: Rapid or sudden attainment of their goals. Advances in their chosen career. Reading could be pertaining to outer space; astrology, astronomy, astronauts, satellites, space shuttles.

Star + King Pentacles: Reached their desired goal of having a large sum of money saved. Could be things like stocks and bonds, retirement accounts savings. They have a nice nest egg.

Star (rev)+ 4 Cups: Very disappointed that they did not achieve their cherished goal. They aren't satisfied with this particular goal or career because it's not what they wished for themselves.

Moon + 7 Cups: Mental illness with auditory and visual hallucinations or un-real imaginings. Possible schizophrenia. Dementia where they don't know what is real or what is happening.

Moon + 5 Wands: Severe mental anxiety and strain. Need to watch out or can lead to a mental or nervous breakdown.

Moon + Strength: A nocturnal animal that comes out at night. Could mean they are afraid of the dark, if taking the reverse of the Strength card. As usual, interpretations are influenced by other cards in the reading.

Moon (rev) + Justice: Examinations or tests regarding mental illness. Court certified mentally ill. Could be exams or biopsy of a tumor or growth (anything round). Tests (or biopsies) done related to growths, a mass, warts, moles, polyps or tumors.

Sun + 6 Swords: Taking a trip or a cruise in the summer. Taking a trip to a sunny location such as a beach or a sunny State. Taking a trip for your birthday.

Sun + Page Pentacles: Child support for or giving money to a baby. Gifts to the baby. A birthday gift.

Sun + 3 Pentacles: Working outside in the sun or at the beach. Really happy about their job because it gives them a sense of freedom with autonomy and of being unrestricted.

Sun (rev) + King Cups: Seeing a doctor due to depression. Their father or husband is depressed. Father or husband has a heat stroke or fever. Remember, you can always come up with new definitions for the cards.

Judgement + Ace Wands: Enjoying good, vibrant health and indicates they will live. They are alive. Energy work promotes good health and healing. Having a full recovery.

Judgement + 10 Pentacles: Renovations of a house or other building. A place people go for things like exercise, dance, yoga, or rehabilitation. A gym. Exercise room.

Judgement + 2 Wands: Full recovery or overcoming adversities and looking forward to new prospects and feeling confident in their future.

Judgement (rev) + 5 Swords: Poor health is causing them difficulties. Or, the item in question (house, car, equipment etc.) is not in new or pristine condition and someone is trying to get the ruse over on them or they will have a lot of difficulties with it.

World + 3 Wands: International business. Starting an importing and exporting business. Moving the business overseas.

World + 4 of Swords: A thing finally completed and now they can rest easy. Resting after a long flight or interstate travel.

World + Death: It is completed and finished; finally done and over. Their flight or trip overseas (or interstate travel) has been blocked; they can't go.

World (rev) + Ace Wands (rev): Something in flight falls from the sky either on fire or due to explosion. Indicates a plane crash; as unfortunate as that is. Ace of Wands can be upright and still indicate fire or explosion.

Swords

Ace Swords + Star: A positive and promising career. An intelligent and sharp minded person who is realizing their hopes and dreams. Any situation will look good with either of these cards in the layout. They get what they desire. Positive attitude about their career or future.

Ace Swords + Lovers: A positive and uplifting relationship. Two intelligent people come together on a venture, regardless of sex or romance. Lovers can just be two people who share the same goals and in agreement.

Ace Swords + 2 Pentacles: Using intellect to weigh or deliberate the matter. Feeling very positive towards two equally attractive options. If there was an accident, this combo suggests a cable or wire was cut.

Ace Swords (rev) + Death: The end of a hostile, negative or threatening situation. A violent and dangerous situation ends in death. Always look at other cards to help determine interpretations.

2 Swords + 8 Pentacles: They made a decision to go back to school, or to read or to write something. This could be job training that leads them to change their position.

2 Swords + 8 Wands (rev): The change has stalled for some reason. Or, what would have been a change isn't happening or going forward. Or, there has been a decision that is delaying the progress –for now.

2 Swords + 8 Swords: A decision or change has restricted them in some manner. Everything has changed because they had to go to jail. A decision they are being forced to make because they have no choice.

2 Swords (rev) + 5 Wands: A poor decision or negative change that they are worried about or putting a lot of mental effort in to.

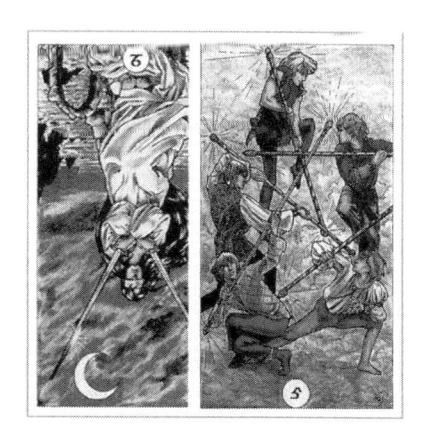

3 Swords + 3 Cups (rev): A lot of people are involved in an accident or are killed. Firing of a lot of people. As horrible as it is, the murder of several woman. A serial killer.

3 Swords + Empress: Miscarriage. Abortion. C-Section. Hysterectomy. Gastric bypass. Abdominal surgery. The mother, elder relative, or infant has a serious accident, maybe even death. Or, mother or elder has a heart attack, heart surgery, serious injury.

3 Swords + Page Pentacles: Cutting off child support or allowance. No longer doling out money to the child. Or, cut off any fees or payments (food stamps?). Severance payments that comes in installments.

3 Swords (rev) + Death (rev): They weren't killed but are left with a long term chronic illness. Or, they did not cut ties or separate and are stuck in a stagnant situation that is going nowhere. Nothing changes.

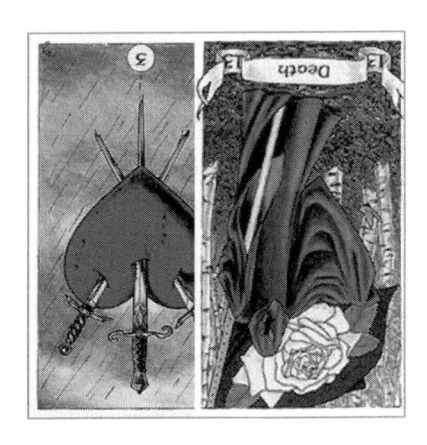

4 Swords + 10 Pentacles: A house of rest. Their bedroom. A hotel or motel. A vacation home. Place of meditation. Having peace in the home.

4 Swords + Page Wands: Sleeping with the radio or television on. Listening to meditation music to help them sleep. Snoring or talking in their sleep. A lot of noise going on while they try to sleep.

4 Swords + Devil: Sleeping pills. Knocked out while on drugs or alcohol. There is something toxic related to their bed or bedroom that is making them sick (could be mold or other allergens).

4 Swords (rev) + 7 Cups (rev): Sleep is disturbed due to nightmares. Exposed to toxic fumes, gases, dusts, dander, or smoke while they sleep. Overcome by smoke while they slept. Smoking in bed.

5 Swords + Judgement: Overcoming the negative intent to do harm or the treachery of another. A peeping tom spying on a naked woman.

5 Swords + 4 Wands (rev): Difficulties in the marriage, either from the inside or from the outside where someone else is causing the relationship to have problems. Someone is trying to destroy their plans.

5 Swords + 8 Cups: Walking away and leaving a difficult situation behind. Leaving the scene of the crime. Making off with something that doesn't belong to them. Leaving something behind that is meant to do harm.

5 Swords (rev) + 9 Wands: Intent to do harm was prevented when someone took a defensive stance. Standing up to a bully.

6 Swords + Tower: Driving into bad weather or disaster. Headed towards a disaster that has already happened, maybe to help out. They think they are leaving a troubled situation behind but are really headed into more of a disaster.

6 Swords + Moon: Driving at night (by the light of the moon). Moon card could show there is some confusion regarding the trip. Maybe their lose their way, or become disoriented.

6 Swords + 7 Swords: Taking a trip or returning back in order to commit a crime. Or, someone is stalking them; going where they are going. Could also be a private investigator tailing them.

6 Swords (rev) + Knight Wands: They don't get to go on the first trip but they do get to take another trip. 6 of Swords is usually a shorter trip compared to Knight of Wands.

7 Swords + 10 Pentacles: Theft or burglary of their house or of a building.

*10 Pents+Chariot=garage (a room for a car)

Swords + 9 Pentacles (rev): Burglary of an area that is not secured. Personal property stolen (purse, jewelry, credit cards, furnishing, artwork). This is not a safe place to be due to criminal activity.

7 Swords + Lovers: Lover is cheating on them. Lover is jealous and possessive. Sexual pervert. Rapist. A masochist. A stalker. Pedophile. Pornography. Sex trafficking. A pimp.

7 Swords (rev) + King Cups: This male is very deceitful and two faced. He says one thing yet intends on doing another. He is "slick" and means to get over on others, yet appears trustworthy and respectable.

8 Swords + 4 Wands: They were forced into the relationship or the marriage. They currently feel trapped in the relationship or marriage.

8 Swords + 8 Wands: Sudden freedom. An escape. Where they were trapped or stymied before they now experience rapid advances and progress.

8 Swords + 7 Pentacles (rev): They go to jail and as a result, lose their job. Or, they can't get a job because of their prison/jail record. Or, they won't let them into the work release program while in jail.

8 Swords (rev) + 6 Cups: There are no restrictions or controls placed on the children. Undisciplined children. Or, kids are freed from a previous stifling type of environment; maybe able to be more themselves now.

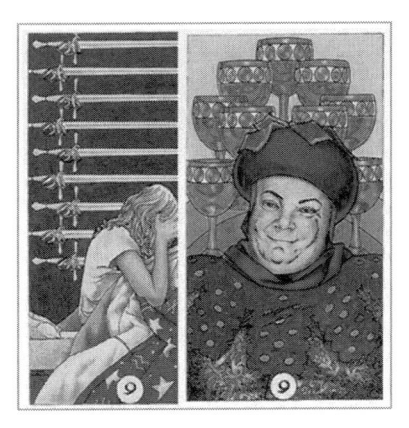

9 Swords + 9 Cups: Putting on a brave face. They are really very hurt and crying but appear to be happy and okay. Or, someone is trying to put on a brave face for the person who is upset in order to make them feel better. Many times the 9 of Cups means unhappiness even if upright.

9 Sword + 4 Pentacles: Crying about something that they just won't let go of. Holding onto the pain. Or, having pain in their arms, elbows, hands. Arthritis. Tendonitis.

9 Swords + Queen Swords: Seeing a healing touch practitioner, nurse or counselor for emotional or physical pain. Going to the hospital or clinic for pain. A pain clinic.

9 Swords (rev) + Strength: The pet is a great source of healing for them (fur therapy). The pet is their emotional companion. An emotional support animal. Or, the pet is no longer hurting or in pain.

10 Swords + 10 Wands: A back injury that causes them to have difficulty walking. There could be metal in their back, hip, or legs such as pins or rods or other prosthetics.

10 Swords + 10 Cups: An accident that involves an entire family, or an accident that devastates the family.

10 Swords + Page pentacles: Being financially compensated after being devastated or injured. Giving or getting a payment or gift (charity) to help out after being devastated either emotionally or financially.

10 Swords (rcv) + 2 Cups: An agreement that puts an end to a devastating situation. Reconciling. They came through something terrible together and are now friends.

Page Swords + Hermit: Urgent news related to something that has suddenly come to light or a new discovery; could be in the news.

Page Swords + World: Urgent news that travels overseas. News that gets circulated and seen worldwide. Getting news that something is completed. Sudden news that someone is coming from overseas or from out of state.

Page Swords + 7 Cups: This news is false. Or, the news is being totally misunderstood or misrepresented. A false flag event. Fake news.

Page Swords (rev) + Justice: Legal dealings with an unruly child or a delinquent child with behavioral issues. Child going to court. Juvenile court. Probation officer.

Knight Swords + 5 Pentacles: Police responding to an assault or abuse call, or possibly a situation of neglect. Sick with cancer.

Knight Swords + 6 Wands: The hero's welcome. Being appreciated for coming to the rescue. Recognized, honored and respected for rescue service rendered. Could be public acclaim or just a simple hug and thank you.

Knight Swords + 10 Pentacles: Police raids the house. Police are called to the home. Fire department or ambulance come to the home. Or, represents a building where rescue vehicles are kept (police cars, fire trucks).

Knight Swords (rev) + Moon: Anger issues destabilizes and makes them irrational. Anger just below the surface. Mental instability causing anger outbursts. Brain disease that cause anger outbursts (dementia, Alzheimer's, brain cancer or tumors).

Queen Swords + Hierophant: This woman is a foreigner. Or, this woman and a foreigner. A faith healer. Doing something different or unconventional with their healing abilities.

Queen Swords + Empress: This female (air sign or nurse/healer) is pregnant. A clinic or hospital for pregnant women. A pediatric nurse. A geriatric nurse for the elderly. A skilled nursing facility for the elderly.

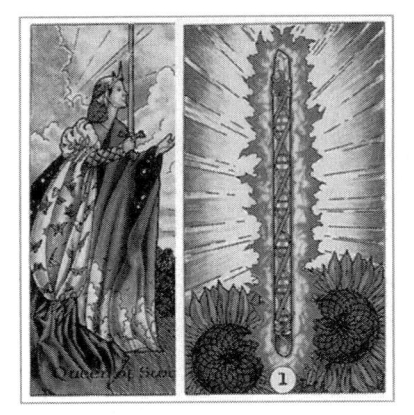

Queen of Swords + Ace Wands: Another way to show this woman is pregnant and will give birth. Fertility clinic. She is a biochemist or geneticist. She is a chemical engineer. This woman is giving "birth" to a brilliant idea or creation.

Queen Swords (rev) + 8 Cups: Walking away from old hurts and mistreatment and leaving it all behind them.

King Swords + 3 Cups: He is associated in some way to a club, restaurant, chef, or even liquor store. He is a bouncer. He drinks alcohol or is an alcoholic. He is a diabetic. He defends these women.

King Swords + Queen Cups: This male (air sign, soldier) has a wife. Look for her if you are wondering if he is married. He could be a cosmetic surgeon with a surgical knife in his hand.

King Swords + 2 Swords: This man is at a crossroads in his life. Or, this man has a decision to make. Could represent that this is the male who will be the one to decide.

King Swords (rev) + 3 Pentacles: An obstinate and neurotic person at work. Can be male or female as long as they display these qualities. This worker has obsessive 'Type-A' personality. Perfectionist or "anal" about their work.

Cups

Ace Cups + 3 Cups: Baby shower. Celebrating the pregnancy. Eating healthy for the pregnancy. Pregnancy diabetes. Or, they are drinking while pregnant. Has a passion for dancing, partying, cooking, eating, or they love several women.

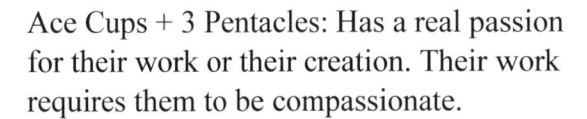

Ace Cups + 3 Pentacles: Has a real passion for their work or their creation. Their work requires them to be compassionate.

Ace of Cups + Page Cups: They really love this child. This is a favorite and special child. This child has a gift of bringing love into other's lives or is very intuitive and creative.

Ace Cups (rev) + 5 Pentacles: Feeling alone and unloved and are being either neglected or abused. They feel rejected. Illness due to fluid overload as in congestive heart failure.

2 Cups + 3 Wands: Making a business agreement. Going into business with a partner or friend. A business merger.

2 Cups + Lovers: They are both friends and lovers. An agreement about sex. Two people really connecting and on the same page, regardless if they are having sex or not.

2 of Cups + 7 Cups (rev): Confusion or misunderstanding regarding an agreement. It isn't want they think it is. Unrealistic expectations of the friendship. Imagining an agreement where there isn't one. Misrepresenting an offer to another. Agreeing to foster or promote an alteration of reality.

2 Cups (rev) + 4 Wands (rev): Can't agree regarding the wedding or a marriage. Rejection of a proposal of marriage. A broken engagement for marriage.

3 Cups + Page Wands: Celebrating an announcement. On stage at a party or club as a singer, dancer, actor, or speaker. A disc jockey. Promoting a gathering, celebration or meeting. Advertising a restaurant or club. Group of people make an announcement.

3 Cups + Sun: A birthday party. A baby shower. Celebrating the birth of a baby. Baby food. A party at the beach or other party in the sun (maybe a pool party).

3 Cups + Devil: Alcoholic drinks. Drinking and drugs at the party. Compulsive eating. Addictions of food, alcohol, or drugs. Where drug addicts gather. The food or drink was spiked or poisoned. Food poisoning.

3 Cups (rev) + 5 Pentacles: Unable to eat or drink because they are sick. The food or drink made them sick. A homeless drunk. An abusive drunk. Their alcohol drinking or drugs is the cause of their illness.

4 Cups + 6 Cups (rev): Very disappointed with the kids or about what is happening with the kids. Sulking over their bad childhood. A disappointed, melancholy or brooding child or sibling.

4 Cups + Page Wands: Broadcasting their displeasure (radio, internet, youtube, skype, phone). Not happy with the radio broadcast, recording, commercial, a proposal, or the promotion of a thing. Which it is depends on feedback from client or surrounding cards.

4 Cup + 2 Swords: Not satisfied with a situation and making a decision to do something about it to change things.

4 Cups (rev) + King Swords (rev): A determined and neurotic male not to be deterred from his mission. A formidable and unrelenting military enemy or terrorist. A very alert and focused neurotic male.

5 Cups + 8 Pentacles (rev): Grief and disappointment over their education, or lack of education. Failed school, or are making bad grades. Regrets what they wrote. Grief caused by documents, letters, emails. 8 of pentacles can be upright or reversed and still mean grief over the school or documents.

5 Cups + 3 Swords: Very tragic accident with probable loss of life. Grief and loss over a death, separation, or divorce. A heart attack or a death brought about by a major grief. Grief or loss is so great that they commit suicide.

5 Cups + Star (rev): Regrets over loss of a cherished goal or of hopes and dreams. Grief over loss of career.

5 Cups (rev) + Knight Cups: Past grief and loss is over and forgotten and a new opportunity or a new romance is in the offering.

6 Cups + 3 Cups: A children's party. Children dancing or playing. A reunion of siblings or cousins. Going out to a restaurant, club or party with siblings. The child is diabetic. The 3 of cups can be upright or reversed to indicate diabetes. Children are drinking alcohol.

6 Cups + Lovers (rev): Child molestations. A pedophile. Statutory rape. Child prostitution or pornography. Children experimenting with sex. The Lovers card can be either upright or reversed and still mean sex or perversion of sex.

6 Cups + 8 Swords: One of the children is going to go to jail, or is in jail. Grounding or restricting the child in some way. Kids are tied up or got trapped. Kidnapped the children. Keeping them from the kids or the kids from them.

6 Cups (rev) + 5 Swords: Problems with a gang of kids or juvenile delinquent activity. Kids making trouble or vandalizing. Kids bullying other kids.

7 Cups + 8 Pentacles: Drawing, doodling, sketching, etching, water coloring, painting, coloring book. An artist. An autographed picture or autographed painting. A book with or about pictures, art, or paintings. Imaginary, fictional or fanciful writings.

7 Cups + 3 Pentacles (rev): Misunderstandings or miscommunication regarding the job. The job isn't what they think it is. Or, they aren't doing the job properly due to poor communication so don't really understand what they are supposed to be doing.

7 Cups + King Swords (rev): A neurotic male who is imagining things or fantasizing. He does not have a good grasp on reality and is dangerous because of that.

7 Cups (rev) + Hermit: Shedding light on or investigating a miscommunication or misunderstanding. Clearing up a misunderstanding. A search light in the fog or smog. Glasses to help their blurry of fuzzy vision.

8 Cups + Hermit: Seeking someone who has left or wandered off. Maybe they got lost and are trying to find their way and are looking for clues. Getting therapy or guidance as they leave a situation behind. A hiking or trail guide. A tour guide.

8 Cups + 8 Wands: Leaving it all behind suddenly. Covering a lot of ground quickly. Making rapid progress or advances in a new direction, new adventure, or enterprise very quickly.

8 Cups + 10 Pentacles: They have left the building or house. You will not find them there. They run away from home. Walking away from the property. Maybe they have set out to find a particular building, or home.

8 Cups (rev) + Ace Swords (rev): They did not leave or walk away and now they are in a very negative and hostile situation, or they are already in a hostile situation but they aren't leaving for some reason.

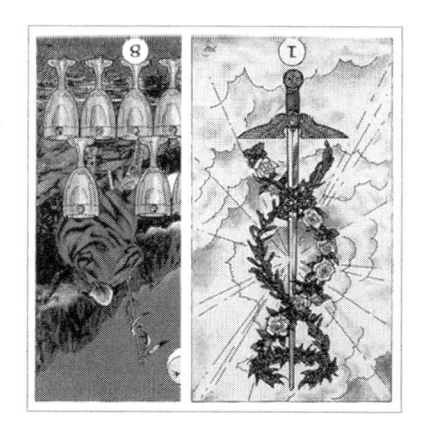

9 Cups + 6 Cups: They get a lot of joy and pleasure out of the children. They feel generous towards the children. The children are happy, or they are friendly, gregarious, or precocious.

9 Cups + 8 Pentacles: They are happy with their school or schoolwork, or their study and training. It is a friendly letter, letters of good referral, thank you notes, invitations. Writing or reading humorous materials.

9 Cups + Emperor: Finding favor with the boss or other person in authority. Friends in high places. Favorable influence with an authority figure.

9 Cups (rev) + Devil: Bipolar or anti-depressant medications (prescribed). Taking illegal drugs because they are depressed. Being unhappy with another or with themselves because of the drug use.

10 Cups + 9 Wands: They are either defending their family or standing up for themselves against their family. The family could be united in a defense.

10 Cups + World: Taking a flight or interstate travel to see their family. Could also be overseas flight. Family members could be coming to see them. Something that involves or unites the entire family.

10 Cups + 4 Wands: A marriage welcomed by the family. Having a large family gathered at a wedding.

10 Cups (rev) + Lovers (rev): A sexual scandal that has turned the family up-sided down. A family of sexual deviants. Incest in the family. The Lovers card could also be upright for sexual deviation, especially if other negative cards are present.

Page Cups + 2 Wands: This child or sibling is confident in their future. They have accomplished previous goals and have a good ego and self-esteem. They are looking forward to something with anticipation. Or, they are waiting and watching for something or someone.

Page Cups + 2 Pentacles (rev): Child takes a fall and injures, sprains, or breaks their ankle, foot, or leg. The child is trying to juggle too many things and is feeling overwhelmed.

Page Cups + Queen Wands (rev): This child cuts off communications. Remember, Page of Cups could be anyone child-like, no matter their age. Could also be one's sibling. This child could be shy and withdrawn, or has fear of social settings; might be autistic.

Page Cups (rev) + Justice: They are legally disabled, whether physically or mentally. They are getting disability insurance. Could also be short or long term disability insurance.

Knight Cups + 4 Pentacles: Very possessive lover. Wanting to hang onto a romantic relationship. If not a relationship, then represents an opportunity or offering. Then it would be wanting to keep this opportunity or offering for themselves and away from others.

Knight Cups + Page Wands: Lover proposes. Announcing an engagement. Prospects or opportunity for buying and selling. Dating websites. Pursing a love interest through multimedia avenues like the internet, Skype, phone, texting.

Knight Cups + Emperor (rev): Their romantic partner is very dominating and controlling (male or female).

Knight Cups (rev) + 8 Swords (rev): An unfaithful lover who won't commit. They feel free to take their romance elsewhere. Sense of freedom that comes when a bad relationship ends.

Queen Cups + 3 Cups (rev): The mother or wife is an alcoholic. The mother or wife is diabetic. They party excessively. They have problems with eating, or shows that they don't have groceries.

Queen Cups + Page Wands: Communication with their mother or wife. A pretty woman who sings, preforms on stage, does television shows, commercials, magazine or ads. The advertisement of beauty products.

Queen Cups + 6 Wands: A caring woman, wife or mother, who is being appreciated. A woman famous for her beauty who is idolized by the public. A "star". A famous model. A prominent woman in society. This water sign woman will be triumphant in the end.

Queen Cups (rev) + 5 Swords: Being stabbed in the back and taken advantage of by a deceitful or gossiping woman. Troubles out of the ex-wife or a problem mother.

King Cups + Knight Wands: The husband or father travels or they move. The husband or father takes trips or is a truck driver. This man deals in horses or cattle.

King Cups + Ace Wands (rev): This man is not their biological father. This man is sterile, infertile. This man is involved with a fire or explosive; either as victim or perpetrator.

King Cups + 8 Pentacles: This male is their teacher or instructor. Or, he is helping them learn to read, write, or helps them study and do their homework. The father or father figure reads to them The husband or father is in school or training. Training as a doctor.

King Cups (rev) + 5 Pentacles: Their father or husband is abusive. Their father or husband is injured or sick, or maybe homeless.

Wands

Ace Wands + 8 Swords: Having a brilliant and creative idea but are being prohibited from realizing it. Only if other negative cards are present (3 swords, 5 cups, Tower) can we say that they were trapped in a fire or explosion.

Ace Wands + 7 Cups: Imagining or faking that they are pregnant. A false pregnancy. Daydreaming about being pregnant. Smoke from a fire. Cigarette smoke. Explosion that causes smoke. What the peat-moss fires of Russia looked like in July 2010.

Ace Wands + Ace Pentacles: A creative endeavor that brings them a lot of money.

Ace Wands (rev) + Knight Swords (rev): A fire or explosion set by anger. Chemotherapy and/or radiation for cancer. Reversed Ace Wands can be antibiotics (against life) or chemo. Reversed Knight Swords can be anger or cancer.

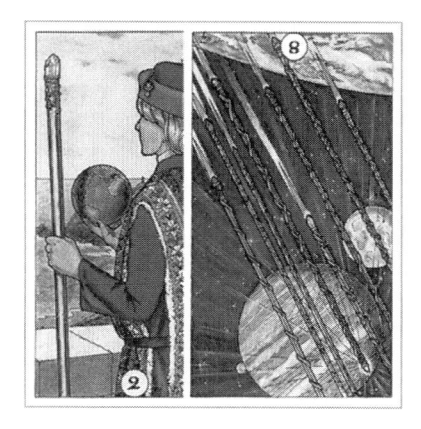

2 Wands + 8 Wands (rev): Watching and waiting for something, meanwhile things are being delayed and not advancing. Or, they look forward to and are ready for something that doesn't seem to be happening.

2 Wands + Star: Good prospects for the future and of reaching their goals. They will achieve what it is they set out to do in the world.

2 Wands + 10 Wands: Pursuing the goals that they are eager to obtain is going to take a lot of hard work. They seem to be willing to do it.

2 Wands (rev) + 9 Cups (rev): They are in a bad place, feeling like they can't do anything right and might say things like, "what's the use?". Their confidence is low and they aren't liking themselves right now. Hopefully, this will pass.

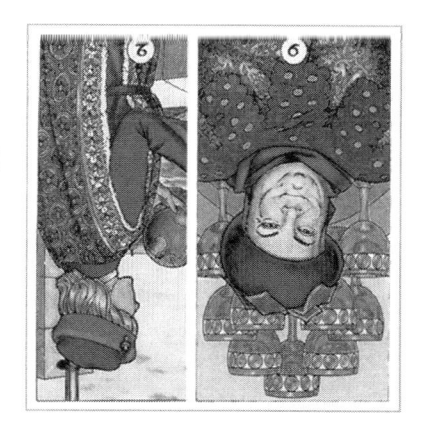

3 Wands + Emperor: The owner, president, or CEO of a business. Going into business with a powerful person who is in a position of authority.

3 Wands + 3 Cups: Business party. Company picnic. Business that deals with food or drink; a club, a restaurant, fast food, grocery store, catering business, party supplies. A dance studio. Or, looking to network with a groups of others.

3 Wands + 7 Swords: A crooked business deal. Company theft. Employees might be stealing. A spy or saboteur within the company. Theft of equipment, business plans, theft of contacts, or other information.

3 Wands (rev) + Wheel of fortune: The turnaround or reversal of misfortune with a business. Or, the business problems or demise turns out to be a very fortunate thing. Maybe they got out in time or the business failure leads to something even better.

4 Wands + 8 Cups (rev): This couple has no adventures together and don't go anywhere together. Or, they don't walk away from the marriage. They salvage what is left of the marriage.

4 Wands + 9 Pentacles: They marry well. They feel secure and confident in their marriage. Getting married in a type of garden setting or luxurious setting. A very elaborate wedding.

4 Wands + 8 Wands (rev): Their wedding is being delayed. It still might occur later. Their marriage is stagnant. Joint ventures are being delayed.

4 Wands (rev) + 5 Pentacles: An ended marriage or relationship leads to poverty or homelessness. An abusive marriage. Marriage strained or ended due to illness. Foundation issues with house or building.

5 Wands + Knight Swords (rev): They are worried about cancer, or they are worried about someone's anger. Or, they lash out in anger due to worry or mental stress.

5 Wands + Temperance (rev): A lot of worry is exhausting them and they are energetically off balanced. They are completely stressed out and exhausted. Watch out for nervous breakdown.

5 Wands + Death: Worried about death or the end of something. More likely reads as an end to their worry.

5 Wands (rev) + 9 Pentacles: They are not worried about the environment as it appears to be safe and secure. Or, they aren't worried about their financial security as it appears they can live very comfortably and possibly luxuriously.

6 Wands + 8 Pentacles: A well-known and recognized writer. Getting recognition and honor for what they write. A book signing. An autograph of a famous person. An autobiography.

6 Wands + 4 Pentacles: They are trying to hold onto and safe keep their reputation. Trying to hang onto their fame in a possessive way ("mine"). A famous person going into seclusion and away from the public eye.

6 Wand + 4 Cups: They are not happy with the recognition, fame, or honor given (probably of another). They are well known for being a moody, sour, and discontented person.

6 Cups (rev) + 7 Pentacles (rev): Their background check (poor character) is keeping them from getting a job. Or, a bad reputation or bad referral is keeping them from getting a job.

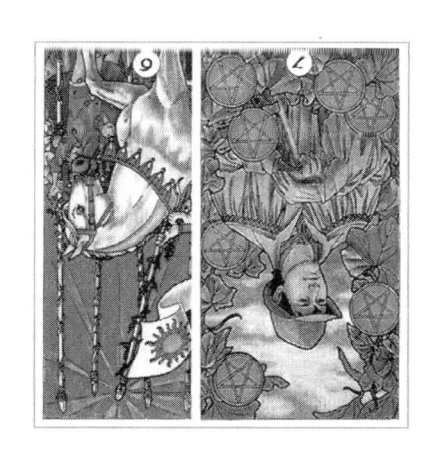

7 Wands + Empress: A successful pregnancy. Success in caregiving, maybe in finding a babysitter, or nursing home.

7 Wands + Judgement: Congratulations, they have gained triumph and success. They have come "through the fire" smelling like a rose. Successful return to good health or item restored to like new working order.

7 Wands + Devil (rev): Overcoming a drug, alcohol, or smoking addiction. Overcoming anything that was not healthy or was toxic for them, including bad relationships.

7 Wands (rev) + Ace Cups (rev): Unsuccessful and alone. They were not successful in obtaining someone's love. Was not able to get pregnant or sustain the pregnancy.

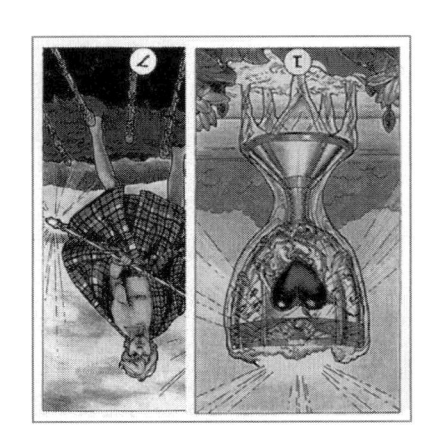

8 Wands + Wheel of Fortune: Good fortune, growth, and advancement. Fortune that comes quickly. Their quick action leads to good fortune.

8 Wands + 5 Wands: A fast and quick thinker and problem solver. Quick on their feet and agile minded. Worrying about how they are going to make progress or these advances are causing them worry.

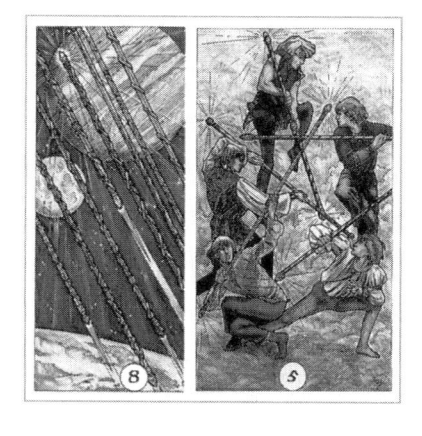

8 Wands + Hierophant: Giving thanks to God in prayer for the advances, promotion, or progress made. Making rapid progress in relation to religion or the church.

8 Wands (rev) + Hanged man: Progress has been suspended or delayed. Advances are in limbo and not going forward at this time. This could be a temporary situation. If it were indeed the end and not just a delay, there would be the Death card.

9 Wands + 9 Cups (rev): They are on the defensive and very unhappy. They aren't angry but more depressed yet ready to make a stand to defend themselves. Or, someone is unhappy about the position they have taken, maybe they want them to be on their side but they are against them.

9 Wands + 5 Pentacles: Defending those who they think is less fortunate. Standing up for the homeless or poor. Defending themselves against an abusive situation.

9 Wands + 5 Swords: Defending themselves and standing up to a bully or to someone trying to take advantage of them. Could be that by taking this defensive stance they are causing a lot of trouble for others.

9 Wands (rev) + 5 Cups (rev): They have put their guard down and have no regrets. They are basically over it. It doesn't matter to them anymore, one way or the other.

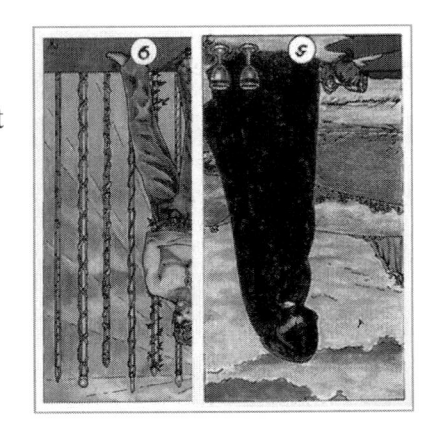

10 Wands + Sun (rev): They are carrying a heavy burden that is making them depressed. Maybe they are working long hours due to depression because it keeps them preoccupied. Walking or jogging in the heat.

10 Wands + King Pentacles: They worked hard and now have a nice savings account or 401K.

10 Wands + Lovers (rev): Their working long hours is hurting their relationship and intimacy with their partner. Could be that because of their long hours, their significant other is cheating on them.

10 Wands (rev) + Towers: Irresponsibility resulted in disaster. Somebody wasn't doing their job. Not taking on this responsibility or burden will lead to disaster. They are not taking responsibility for the disaster, or in fact they are not responsible for the disaster.

Page Wands + Chariot: Buying or selling a vehicle. Noise or music coming from a vehicle. A car radio. A salesman. An auction where vehicles are sold.

Page Wands + 9 Cups: Telling or hearing something that makes them laugh or that they think is funny. Or, maybe it makes them very happy. A stand-up comedian. A comedy play or television show.

Page Wands + Strength: Calling to an animal or pet. The pet answers to commands. Tracking device on the pet. Hearing an animal that is making a noise; such as barking, crowing, scratching, chewing.

Page Wands (rev) + Tower: No alarm went out before disaster struck (tornado, earthquake, tsunami, flood, fire). Smoke alarms didn't work. Communications cut off due to disaster.

Knight Wands + 8 Swords: Action is being prohibited. Being taken to jail or other detention. Detainees, prisoners, hostages, or kidnapped victim are being moved from one location to another.

Knight Wands + Knight Cups: Moving to take advantage of an opportunity. Or, moving to pursue a romantic relationship.

Knight Wands + 3 Swords: Not a good idea to take this trip or move because it leads to a horrible accident, injury or even death. Or, this move cuts them off completely, severing all connections whether they intend to or not.

Knight Wands (rev) + High Priestess: Forced action to expose secrets or confidential information. Being forced to give up passwords, secret documents, their own or other's personal information like social security, bank accounts; anything that should be kept private or personal.

Queen Wands + World: This woman (fire sign, or red haired) is an international. Or, she flies from, or to, overseas. Or, something this woman was working on is completed.

Queen Wands + Page Swords: This woman hears urgent news. Getting news from or about this woman. This woman is a reporter, journalist, or newscaster. A woman who is rash in her behavior (taking reversed meaning of Page of Swords).

Queen Wands + Ace Swords: This woman exhibits a very positive attitude. Or, she is very intelligent, with sharp mind. If taking the reverse of Ace of Swords, then she has a sharp and cutting tongue and is critical.

Queen Wands (rev) + Ace Wands (rev): A socially isolated woman who suffers depression likely due to chemical imbalance. Or, she could be going through chemo or radiation treatments.

King Wands + Hierophant: A charismatic religious personality. A television or radio evangelist. A stage or pulpit preacher. Or, a man with pious, strong religious morals and ethics. Or, this male is gay (taking the reverse of Hierophant meaning anything going against religious tradition).

King Wands + Knight Pentacles: This man offers help, either financially or with other assistance. If King of Wands represents the client, then he gets a loan or credit card.

King Wands + Page Cups: Two individuals, this man and this child. This male and a young sibling. Could mean it is the man's biological child (page cups).

King Wands (rev) + Knight Swords (rev): An obnoxious male (or ex) is very angry. Or, they are very angry with this obnoxious male. This obnoxious male might attack them out of anger.

Pentacles

Ace Pentacles + 9 Pentacles: Money brings financial security. Large amount of money MADE or SPENT related to luxury items; furniture, clothing, perfumes, jewelry, paintings. Could be financial gains made through providing outdoor services such as landscaping, gardening, or as a florist.

Ace Pentacles + 8 Wands: Rapid attainment of wealth. Wealth and attainment together. Promotion or other advances that leads to a lot of money. Large amount of money spent towards rapid advancements.

Ace Pentacles + Page Wands: Money behind the media; radio or television. Well paid speaker, singer, performer, actor, or promoter. Money for sales of computers, electronics, or multimedia. Stock market. Auctions.

Ace Pentacles (rev) + 7 Swords: Theft of a lot of money. Loss of money through deception or sabotage. Someone commits or plans to commit assault and battery. Destruction of property.

2 Pentacles + 4 Pentacles: Deliberating on two or more items while wanting them both (or all). Has two but won't share. Wiring money to a location away from prying eyes in a secured place, like a secret account.

2 Pentacles + Ace Wands: They trip or fall and sprain or strain something; more likely their foot, ankle or leg. They might even break something. Ace of wands can represent inflammation, or broken bone. A live electrical wire. WiFi.

2 Pentacles + Tower: Trying to stay balanced or juggle multiple things (many hats) during a disaster. A hurricane or tornado. Any cyclic weather related disaster (el-Nina).

2 Pentacles (rev) + Chariot: Regaining control after being thrown off balance. Unbalanced tires. Broken struts. Car wears the tires; possible bent frame. Problem with cables, belts or wiring of the vehicle. Steering problems.

3 Pentacles + 10 Pentacles: Working from home. Working on the house. Their job involves houses, or buildings, such as realtor, construction, cleaning services, carpentry, roofer, etc'.

3 Pentacles + 3 Cups: They work in the food industry; waiters, cook, chef, restaurant, caterer. They work in a club, bartender, dancer. Their work involves parties, celebrations. There is a party at their job. Company picnic.

3 Pentacles + 9 Cups: They are very happy about their job. This is a job they will like. Their job involves being friendly and helpful. They are a greeter.

3 Pentacles (rev) + 2 Wands (rev): Having lost their job has upset their confidence and self-esteem. Their job causes them to feel bad about themselves. Lack of future potential or prospects with their work.

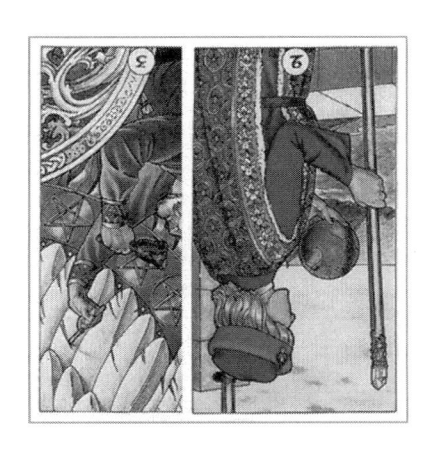

4 Pentacles + 5 Pentacles: Injury to arms, elbows, hands. Arthritic disease. Being both possessive and abusive towards someone.

4 Pentacles + Tower: Preparing to ride out a disaster by sheltering themselves. Storing things like food, water. A place of safety, like a shelter during disaster. What a survivalist or "Prepper" might look like.

4 Pentacles + 10 Pentacles: Being possessive of the house; wanting to keep it for themselves. Can also mean a safe-house. Maybe they want to stay at this house and not be asked to leave. A squatter.

4 Pentacles (rev) + 9 Swords (rev): Has let go of issues that used to emotionally hurt them so are not crying in pain anymore. No more tears, all is forgiven. No more pain in arms or hands.

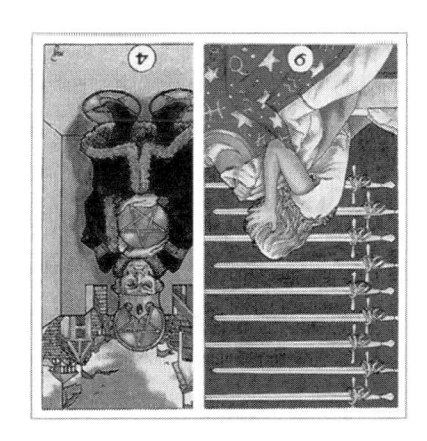

5 Pentacles + Knight Wands (rev): An illness or injury that affects the neuromuscular system or their ability to move. Injury caused by an incident with a horse. Abuse of horse or other large animals. The large animal is ill or injured.

5 Pentacles + Moon: All forms of mental illness (Alzheimer's, stroke, amnesia, schizophrenia, manic depressive, dementia). Homelessness born out of mental illness. Abuse of the mentally ill. Abuse caused the mental disturbance.

5 Pentacles + 5 Swords: The illness or injury was intentional and the result of a deliberate act. A very difficult illness to endure.

5 Pentacles (rev) + Judgement: Having overcome an illness or injury to a full recovery and back to good health.

6 Pentacles + Star: Receives assistance with their goals or dreams. Being able to make their ends meet and have enough left over to pursue their dream.

6 Pentacles + 7 Swords: Giving comes with ulterior motives. There are strings attached. Paying someone to do a criminal or sneaky act. A hired assassin, thief, or saboteur. A hired spy or private investigator.

6 Pentacles + 4 Cups: Disgruntled that they are having to give out their money, either to bills or to others. Or, this person isn't satisfied with what is being given to them.

6 Pentacles (rev) + 2 Cups (rev): A friendship or agreement has ended or is having problems because assistance is not being given. Neither giving assistance or coming to an agreement. Doling out stops, so friendship stops.

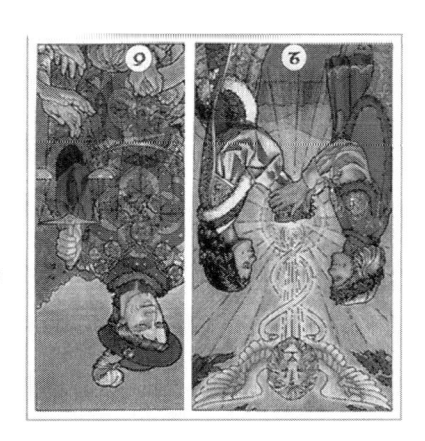

7 Pentacles + 10 Wands: Working very hard on their feet for long hours, or carrying heavy loads. A lot of walking or lifting is involved in their job. Or, they carry the majority of the responsibility on the job.

7 Pentacles + World: Their job will take them overseas. Their work involves many continents or interstate travel. Their job is as a pilot or stewardess.

7 Pentacles + 3 Pentacles: They have two jobs or will acquire a second job. Moonlighting (having a second job).

7 Pentacles (rev) + Hermit (rev): Unemployed and not seeking a job. Unable to work due to poor eyesight or because of old age. Or, the job suffers due to lack of proper supervision or guidance.

8 Pentacles + 6 Cups: Children who are studying, in school, or in training. An elementary school. Writing to the children or about their childhood. Teaching or tutoring children. A child's classroom. Reading to children.

8 Pentacles + 4 Swords: Reading or studying in bed. Reading to another or being read to by another while in bed. Could be listening to an audio book while in bed.

8 Pentacles + 7 Swords: Notes or letters with ill intent to do harm. The poison pen letter. Counterfeiting. Stealing documents. Forged documents or signature. Faking a copy. A forgery.

8 Pentacles (rev) + Fool: Illiterate, uneducated person. Document problems that they aren't involved with or aren't aware of. They are being gullible of fooled about faked documents.

9 Pentacles + 6 Wands: Wealthy, well known and respected. A rich and elegant celebrity. Respected because of their wealth. Royalty. Upper class.

9 Pentacles + 4 Swords: Having financial security brings them peace of mind. Having a safe and secure, or comfortable place to sleep.

9 Pentacles + 5 Swords: Living off other people's finances because they feel they deserve it or feel it is owed to them. Taking advantage a woman who is well off or because they think she is well off. Stealing from her in a sneaky way.

9 Pentacles (rev) + Strength (rev): Loss of financial security brings fear or paranoia. They are in an unsecured, unsafe environment and are afraid.

10 Pentacles + 3 Cups: Having a party or celebration at their house. Dinner or drinks at a restaurant, hotel, or in their room. A dance studio. A café or cafeteria. The kitchen. Conference room for meetings with other people.

10 Pentacles + Queen Swords: A clinic or hospital building. A building or office where one goes for healing. In reference to this woman's home or office. She could be a nurse, Reiki person or other type of healer working from a building, office, or home.

10 Pentacles + 5 Pentacles: Abuse happening in the home. A home for the abused, sick, or homeless. The house or building is making them sick. The house itself is damaged in some way.

10 Pentacles (rev) + Strength: Having a problem with the house related to animals or insects (spiders, moles, ants, termites, squirrels, roaches). Homeless animal. Or, a rescue pet that had no home or lost its home.

129

Page Pentacles + Wheel Fortune: A winning ticket. Winning the lottery. A small amount paid for huge returns or brings good fortune. Having to split the inheritance or fortune; they only get a part of it.

Page Pentacles + Knight Pentacles: Taking a small amount of money and compounding it into a much larger amount, like dividends.

Page Pentacles + Justice: Insurance payments. Attorney fees. Taxes to the state or government offices. Fees you are legally bound to make. Garnished wages. Court ordered child support.

Page Pentacles (rev) + 3 Cups: Unable to buy food or drinks. No money for ticket or fee to go to the celebration or party. Not getting or giving a gift at the party. If page pentacles were upright, then it could be read as food stamps.

Knight of Pentacles + Fool: Getting assistance (financial or otherwise) to start something new. Getting a loan to start anew. Getting a new loan or new credit card.

Knight Pentacles + 6 Wands (rev): Not being appreciated or given recognition for the financial or other assistance that was given.

Knight Pentacles + Chariot: Received a bank loan or other financing or credit on a vehicle. Getting a title loan against their vehicle.

Knight Pentacles (rev) + 4 Cups: A totally unmotivated and lazy person who is discontented in general. Sulking that they didn't get the money, credit card, or other support they wanted.

Queen Pentacles + Hermit: This woman gives good advice or guidance. She could be an earth-sign woman, of ethnic heritage, or dark skinned. Or, they are seeking to find this woman.

Queen Pentacles + Sun: This earth-sign woman is pregnant, or it is her birthday. She could also be ethnic or dark skinned. She goes to the beach or lives in a sunny location. She is free-spirited or maybe even a nudist.

Queen Pentacles + Hierophant: This woman is very religious, she prays a lot or goes to church. This woman is praying for you, or you are praying for her. She manages a religious affiliation or church. Or, she is a foreigner, or she may be gay.

Queen Pentacles (rev) + Moon: Financial crisis causes mental confusion or other mental instability. Maybe they don't know how to handle the situation. This woman (earth-sign, ethnic, or dark skinned or hair) is mentally ill.

King Pentacles + World: International banking. Money in the bank overseas. An earth-sign male flies overseas or travels interstate. Having reached the conclusion of an ultimate financial goal

King Pentacles + 10 Pentacles: Bank loan for a house or other building or office. A home equity loan or line of credit. Or, they have both a savings and a home.

King Pentacles + 3 Swords: Completely cut off from the bank account or finances. Or, this earth sign male dies, has surgery, heart attack, or serious accident. Or, this earth sign male is the perpetrator who seriously harms someone.

King Pentacles (rev) + Knight Swords (rev): Anger about financial losses. This earth sign male is angry or has cancer. Liver cancer. Knight of swords can be upright or reversed for both cancer or anger.

Three Card Combinations

Major

Fool + 2 Wands + 9 Cups:

Looking forward to new beginnings and goals that they are happy about.

Fool + 5 Wands + 3 Pentacles

They are worried about starting a new job or worried that they don't have the experience necessary to do the job.

Fool (rev) + Justice + Devil

The legal system is involved with a disabled child and their medications. Or, legal system involved with something stupid someone did regarding drugs.

Fool (rev) + 6 Cups + 8 Swords

Kids do a stupid and foolish thing that lands them in jail or on probation. Or, they did a stupid thing in their childhood that they went to jail for.

Magician + 2 Swords + Justice

An expert in their field making a legal decision. "In their professional opinion". Having the knowledge, skill and experience to make an equitable decision that is right and fair. A legal mediator.

Magician + Emperor + 10 Swords

The rugged, bearded (handsome?) leader is dead. Layout in regards to query of Osama Bin Laden on 2/16/10 when his picture was on the cover of Forbes magazine (he was already dead - and had been dead).

Magician (rev) + Ace Pentacles (rev) + 3 Wands (rev)

Poor craftsmanship leads to mechanical failure (rev ace pents) or leads to business financial losses.

Magician (rev) + 5 Swords + Queen Cups (rev)

Using black magic to harm either the ex-wife, their mother, or a gossiping woman. Or, this woman is doing the black magic.

High Priestess + Queen Wands + 8 Pentacles

This fire sign woman writes things of a confidential nature, or writes things in secret. She is a psychic reader, studies, or goes for training and seminars. A secrete file on her.

High Priestess + 6 Cups (rev) + 5 Pentacles

Keeping secret, or hidden information about childhood abuse, neglect or poverty.

High Priestess + 5 Swords + 7 Wands

Spilling the beans, exposing secrets, with ill intent to get the upper hand. Or, they succeed by stooping to these underhanded measures.

High Priestess (rev) + Strength (rev) + Hermit

They are afraid about something secret being exposed or investigated.

Empress + Page Wands + 4 Wands

A pregnant woman announces her wedding. Or, an elder relative announces her wedding.

Empress + 5 Cups + Page Swords

Receiving urgent news about the loss of the pregnancy or the baby. Or, news that brings grief about the loss of an elder relative, or mother.

Empress (rev) + Hanged Man) + Death

The pregnancy is ended due to umbilical cord around the neck or baby aspirates the amniotic fluid.

Empress (rev) + Queen Swords + Judgement

Problems with the pregnancy or abdomen causes them to go to the clinic or hospital but they recover to good health.

Emperor + 2 Swords + Death

Person in position of authority makes the decision that is final or puts an end to it.

Emperor + 3 wands + 7 Pentacles

This industrious entrepreneur (Emperor) has both a business and a job.

Emperor (rev) + 5 Swords + 3 Pentacles

An obstinate, rude, and dominating person (or boss) is causing difficulties at work.

Emperor (rev) + Strength (rev) + Lovers

An arrogant person is intimidating (Strength reversed) someone for sex. Be careful it isn't a child.

Hierophant + 4 Swords + 9 Swords

They are praying to or crying to God while in bed.

Hierophant + Knight Cups + Ace cups

Romantic relationship with a foreigner, person of a different race, or with a gay person, that is true love (at least on one person's part).Or, this love interest is pregnant.

Hierophant (rev) + 6 Wands (rev) + 2 Cups (rev)

Not respecting or partnering with, because of culture, race, or because they are gay. Or, they withhold their association because it would damage their own reputation.

Hierophant (rev) + King Cups + 7 Cups

Difference in race, culture, or religion of this male causes a misunderstanding. Or, there is a misperception of them being gay.

Lovers + Ace Cups + Sun

This couple is in love and are going to have a baby. Both Ace Cups and Sun card represent a baby.

Lovers + 5 Pentacles + Ace Wands

A sexually transmitted viral or bacterial infection that could cause burning (candida, herpes). Or, sexual abuse leads to pregnancy.

Lovers (rev) + Queen Cups (rev) + 5 Swords

They have a wife they are cheating on or lying about having. With the Queen upright she does not appear to be the source of the problem.

Lovers (rev) + 7 Swords + 8 Swords

This is a rapist who has been in jail or is going to jail. Or, he is holding someone against their will. Could be sex trafficking or sex slave activity.

Chariot + Page Wands + Knight cups

An opportunity to buy or sell a vehicle(s). An offer or opportunity to get into car sales, maybe as a car salesman or buying a car lot.

Chariot + 2 Swords + Page Cups

Making a decision about getting a car for this kid. Or, controlling any decision for this child so that the child does not have the choice.

Chariot (rev) + 4 pentacles + 7 Swords

The car getting repossessed. Chariot can also be upright. The 4 of pentacles is taking possession, and 7 swords is a sneaky operation or seen as negative action.

Chariot (rev) + Justice + 3 Cups

Legal issues with drinking and driving. License revoked or tickets, or going to court for drunk driving. Or, legal outcome for vehicle related issue is cause for celebration (winning the case).

Strength + King Swords + Page Cups

This male exerts a personal strength of character with calming influence on this child. A man, a child, and a pet.

Strength + Moon + 9 Pentacles

Nocturnal animal moving around outside at night or getting into the garden (9 pents). This would be important to know in case the animal is harmful to human or pet.

Strength (rev) + 5 Pentacles + Fool

They might have a generalized anxiety disorder and don't realize that this is their problem. They don't realize that the animal is sick or injured, or pets needs are being neglected out of ignorance.

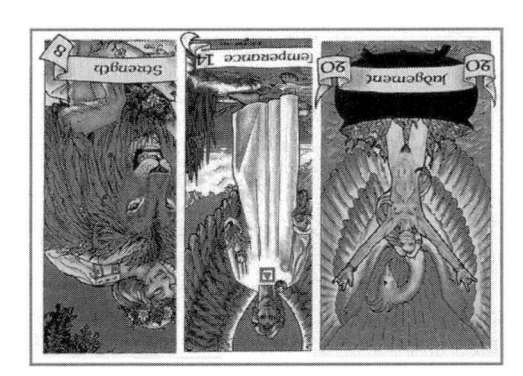

Strength (rev) + Temperance (rev) + Judgement (rev)

Fatigue and exhaustion.
Rev Strength = fatigue
Rev Temperance = stressed,
Rev Judgement = physically down.

Hermit + Fool + Page Swords

Discovering something that they were unaware of before and sending out urgent or amazing news. A discovery that is new and exciting.

Hermit + 7 Cups + 8 Cups

Discovering that something wasn't what it appeared to be or was being misrepresented and then walking away.

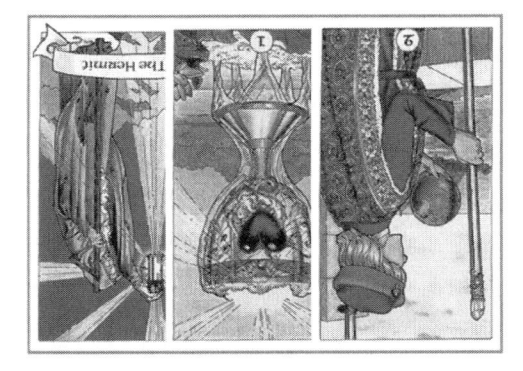

Hermit (rev) + Ace Cups (rev) + 2 Wands (rev)

Feeling lost and without direction (rev hermit) and alone and unloved (rev ace cups). This is causing them to have low self-esteem, self-confidence and poor self-opinion.

Hermit (rev) + 7 Cups + 8 Pentacles (rev)

Difficulty seeing because things are cloudy and not in perspective. This is effecting them in school causing them to have learning difficulties.

Wheel Fortune + Empress + Knight Pentacles

Inheritance from an elder relative, probably a woman but could be male. Could be property but also appears to be a nice sum of money.

Wheel Fortune + Ace Wands + 6 Wands

A creative invention that brings them fame and fortune and recognition.

Wheel Fortune (rev) + Ace Pentacles + Knight Swords

Coming to their financial rescue after a misfortune or loss of fortune.

Wheel Fortune (rev) + Page Wands + 5 Swords

An unfortunate event is being maliciously broadcast. Or, how unfortunate that they said what they did because it is being used against them by their enemies.

Justice + 2 Swords + 2 Cups

A fair and unbiased decision that can be agreed upon. Could be a legal agreement, possible contract, courts, or lawyer involvement.

Justice + 9 Wands + 9 Cups

Very happy that the law or legal system is defending their position. Happy with their legal defense.

Justice (rev) + Hierophant (rev) + 3 Pentacles (rev)

Prejudice and discrimination on the job against someone who is of a different race, religion, is a foreigner, is elderly, or who is gay.

Justice (rev) + 7 Wands + 4 Cups

A legal problem that they overcame successfully, yet they don't appear to be completely satisfied. There was something they wanted that they didn't get.

Hanged Man + Death + 4 Pentacles

A thing in limbo came to an end and they are still in possession of whatever it was they were trying to hang on to. They held on to the very end and are able to keep it.

Hanged Man + 2 Wands + Knight Cups

After a period of things being delayed or suspended, they now look forward to a wonderful opportunity, good prospects, or an offer that is being made.

Hanged Man (rev) + Fool + Moon

Injury due to inexperience or stupid act with some confusion or questions surrounding it. Suggests brain injury, possibly due to hypoxia or choking. Or, mentally disabled due to head or brain injury.

Hanged Man (rev) + 3 Swords + 5 Cups

This is very, very, bad. Life hangs in the balance from serious injury that causes grief. Or, serious head or neck injury, even surgery due to injury.

Death + Strength + Justice

Death of an animal is justified. Taken from reading where driver hit a opossum instead of swerving. Going off the road at that speed would have been disastrous.

Death + Knight Wands + 8 Swords (rev)

End to one's old way of life due to a move that also brings freedom and a release of restrictions or inhibitions.

Death (rev) + 4 Wands + 4 Cups

Stagnant marriage and at least one is not satisfied. Or, they are disappointed that theirs or someone else's marriage didn't end. Or, they don't end their marriage despite not being happy with it.

Death (rev) + Ace Wands + 9 Cups

They don't die, they live. Yea! Or, after a long time (rev Death), they finally get pregnant and are happy. Yea!

Temperance + 7 Wands + Ace Swords

Successfully maneuvered a positive outcome through patience and coordinated actions.

Temperance + Queen Swords + Fool

Evolved spiritual being with gifts of healing upon a spiritual journey. They came into this life with much of their higher-self present with purpose as a spiritual healer.

Temperance (rev) + 3 Pentacles (rev) + 10 Wands

Stress and burnout at their job where they are burdened with hard work and a heavy load.

Temperance (rev) + 5 Pentacles + Death (rev)

Immune system is down causing an illness of a chronic nature, like an auto immune disease.

Devil + 3 Cups + Lovers (rev)

Drugs and sex are at this party. Also suggests someone slipped drugs into a drink or food for date-rape.

Devil + Queen Wands + Strength (rev)

This woman has a fear of germs (devil) or of being poisoned. Or, drugs are causing her to have paranoia or panic attacks.

Devil (rev) + Page Swords (rev) + Page of Cups

Child with behavioral problems (page swords rev) due to drugs. Or, child is on medication to treat behavioral problems.

Devil (rev) + 8 Cups + 4 Swords

Walking away from drugs and having more peace of mind, maybe more rest and sleeping better. Or, they are leaving a negative and toxic situation behind and are relieved.

Tower + 5 Swords + 2 Cups

This disaster was deliberate because two people instigated it. Or, an agreement to take advantage of the disaster. Examples would be price gouging or fake charity.

Tower + 4 Pentacles + 10 Pentacles

Hunkering down in their home during a disaster. From a reading during Russian peat moss fires in July 2010 when people were told to stay indoors.

Tower (rev)+ Knight Swords + Fool

Disaster was diverted because there were those who intervened and most people were never made aware of it (none the wiser).

Tower (rev) +2 Swords + 4 Pent (rev)

A disaster averted brings change and they are able to let it go. Decision to just let it go prevented a disaster. Could be a personal disaster or larger disaster felt by others.

Star + 9 Pentacles + 4 Wands

Realizing their hopes and dreams of financial security in their marriage. They married well.

Star + 7 Cups + Page Wands

Having success in the arena of art, photography, acting, or decorating. Or, they are advertising these things in magazines, commercials radio, magazines, podiums, etc.'

Star (rev) + Tower + 5 Cups

Their hopes and dreams have come crashing down. This is a disaster that dashes their plans and goals and brings them much grief.

Star (rev) + Death + Empress

The end of their career or dreams because they became pregnant, or because they have to care for a child as a baby sitter or they have to care for an elder relative.

Moon + 6 Swords (rev) + 7 Swords

They wait until night to return to commit a crime or steal something. 6 of Swords reversed suggests that they were there before and are returning.

Moon + 4 Swords + 2 Wands

They are mentally at peace. Suggests they were disturbed prior, but now have good ego integrity. Or, they meditate in a kind of self-help exercise to obtain confidence and self-esteem.

Moon (rev) + King Swords (rev) + 5 Wands

A mentally ill, neurotic male that they are worried about because he can be dangerous. Or, a person who is mentally disturbed with an over active mind (5 wands).

Moon (rev) + Hermit + Magician (rev)

Feeble-minded due to old age to the point where they no longer remember their set of skills. Could be Alzheimer's or dementia.

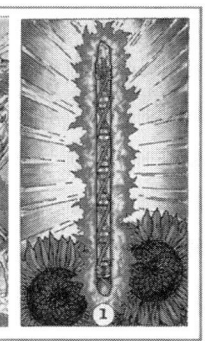

Sun + Ace Cups + Ace Wands

Baby. Baby. Baby. All three of these cards indicate they are going to have a baby and are pregnant; so does Empress card.

Sun + 10 Pentacles + 6 Swords

Having a home in a sunny location near water. Could be beach front property, vacation home, time share. Having a boat-house or travels on the water. Could even "live in a van down by the river".

Sun (rev) + Knight Pentacles (rev) + 8 Pentacles (rev)

They exhibit depression and are being sluggish and lazy (inertia) in school. They aren't even trying.

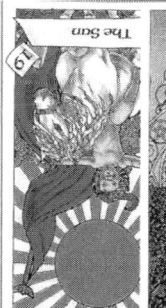

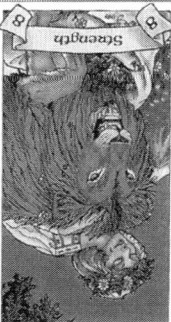

Sun (rev) + 9 Pentacles + Strength (rev)

It is too hot (sun rev) outside (9 pent) for the animal and it is causing them distress.

Judgement + Ace Wands + Magician

A strong magnetic or sexual attraction (ace wands) to a handsome and virile male with a nice physique, maybe he works out (judgement).

Judgement + 3 Cups + 6 Cups

The children are eating healthy foods meant to rejuvenate them. Or, they are eating healthy and exercising, too. Kids are on a health conscious regimen.

Judgement (rev) + Death + 9 Swords

They don't recover. This is the end for them and this upsets the client or other individual.

Judgement (rev) + 3 Pentacles + Page Wands

Taking a broken item and working to fix it or restoring it and then selling it. Fixing and selling electronic items (page wands).

World + King Cups + Queen Swords

A male and female travel the interstate or fly overseas. Or, a doctor who practices in a hospital or clinic overseas (Dr. without borders).

World + 10 Cups + Ace Cups

Feeling fulfilled and complete within a loving family. Their family is now complete because they are having a baby (ace cups).

World (rev) + Page Pentacles (rev) + 4 Pentacles

Some part of it is incomplete because someone is hanging on to part of it. The whole is in pieces and the person with it won't let go.

World (rev) + 4 Swords (rev) + 7 Pentacles

They don't get to travel overseas or interstate because they can't take a vacation or get time off and have to work at their job instead.

7 Swords + Blank + 7 Pentacles

Their criminal history has been expunged (wiped clean) so that they can get a job.

Page Pentacles + Blank + Page Cups

The gifts or payments never made it to the child. Possibly, child support didn't go to the child. Has no record that they made payments to child (payments must go through legal route or there is no proof you paid).

2 Swords + 8 Cups + Blank

Deciding to walk away leaving no trace as to where they went; no forwarding address and no phone number. No one knows where they have gone but they left willingly.

Blank + Hermit + Knight Swords (rev)

Looking for something missing or taken and they are very angry about it. Or, are angry that someone is trying to investigate something that either doesn't exist are they have tried to erase evidence of.

Swords

Ace Swords + Page Swords + 3 Wands

Getting positive news about or getting the 'all clear' to go forward with a business venture; yes you can.

Ace Swords + 3 Pentacles + 8 Wands

Due to having a sharp mind, a positive attitude, or getting a positive performance review at work they get a promotion or make other advances.

Ace Swords (rev) + King Swords + 3 Swords

This soldier is killed in war. This soldier kills others n war. This could be a terroristic attack as an act of war. The rev ace of swords can mean war or hostile, negative situation.

Acc Swords (rev) + 10 Wands + King Swords

Sharp pain in back, leg, or knee, is making it difficult to walk, for which they see a surgeon. Or a soldier (or air sign) received this injury in war.

2 Swords + 4 Pentacles + High Priestess

They have made the decision to keep this under wraps. They are going to play this "close to the chest", keep information of it away from others.

2 Swords + Fool + 7 Wands

The decision to start something new will meet with success. A successful new beginning.

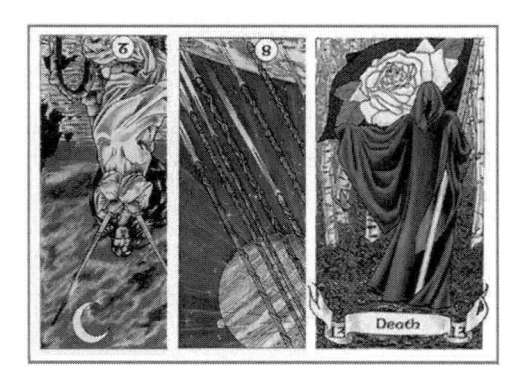

2 Swords (rev) + 8 Wands (rev) + Death

Delaying a decision until the time has passed and the option is no longer available. 8 wands is a time card, upright means fast, reverse mean slow or delay.

2 Swords (rev) + Page Wands (rev) + Wheel of Fortune

They never finalized the decision to make an announcement and this turned out to be very fortunate indeed. It's good they never said it.

3 Swords + Chariot + 6 Cups

Serious vehicular accident involving several young kids. May or may not indicate the death of any of the individuals. More readings are indicated.

3 Swords + Knight Swords + 8 Swords

Stabbing, shooting, serious wounding, or a killing that police respond to where someone goes to jail. Sorry, but 3 of swords is a most gruesomeness card.

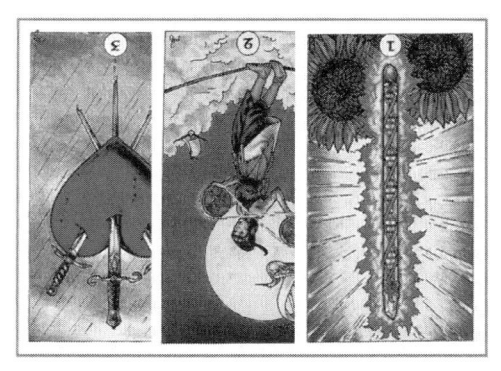

3 Swords (rev) + 2 Pentacles (rev) + Ace Wands (rev)

A cutting wound to the feet that is either inflamed, hot, or infected (or all three). If 3 swords were upright it means their foot was cut off or lost due to infection or explosion.

3 Swords (rev) + Page Wands + Hermit

Accident victim survives and makes whereabouts known by putting out a call or signal whereupon they are found. Could be found due to GPS, tracking device, or black box.

4 Swords + Empress + Judgement

A pregnant woman is put on bed – rest but everything turns out fine. Her and the baby both are unharmed and in good health.

4 Swords + 8 Pentacles + King Wands

All this guy does is sleep and study, sleep and study. Or, he reads in bed, or reads to them in bed. Possible that he is falling asleep in class.

4 Swords (rev) + 3 Cups (rev) + Queen Cups (rev)

Not sleeping or eating properly and is showing up in their appearance; could be too thin, have bags under their eyes, looking tired or older.

4 Swords (rev) + 10 Pentacles (rev) + Ace Cups (rev)

No place to sleep, no family to turn to, and are alone or unloved.
*There is usually a good reason that someone's family would reject them.

5 Swords + Moon + Fool

Taking advantage of and deceiving (moon) a gullible and naïve person. Or, a mentally handicapped (moon+fool) person is being taken advantage of.

5 Swords + Page Pentacles (rev) + Chariot

Someone has removed parts to the car. They are tricking them about parts missing from the car. That part wasn't really added. They aren't really using the money for car payments or repairs; they're lying.

5 Swords (rev) + 7 Wands + 4 Pentacles

They win out over someone who tried to take something from them and they are the ones who wind up with possession of the item.

5 Swords (rev) + Temperance + Knight Swords

A guardian angel or higher being came to their rescue and prevented them from falling victim to harm.

6 Swords + 5 Wands + 6 Pentacles

Things are going more smoothly but they are still worried about making ends meet and paying all their bills. Worried that if they go will they be able to make it.

6 Swords + Hanged Man + 5 Pentacles

Their trip is being postponed due to an injury or illness. Or, they are leaving to be with someone who is very ill.

6 Swords (rev) + Knight Swords (rev) + 4 Cups

Didn't get to go on the trip and are angry about it and are sulking. Or, they refuse to go because they are angry about not getting their way about something.

6 Swords (rev) + 7 Swords + 10 Pentacles

A criminal is staking out the house. Shows them retuning later (going back the way they came) to break into the house. Always be careful of workers in your home.

7 Swords + 10 Pentacles + Chariot

Breaking in through the garage. A garage is a "house" for the car. Plus, many times thieves can get into the house from the garage.

7 Swords + 9 Pentacles + Page Wands (rev)

Sneaking into a secured area undetected. No one becomes "alarmed" at their presence even if in full sight.

7 Swords (rev) + 3 Cups + Fool

A habitual predator of either young and naïve women, handicapped women, drunk women, or "partying" women in clubs.

7 Swords (rev) + Hermit + Empress

Preying on the elderly. Abusing or preying on the elderly in a nursing home (empress). Hermit could show investigation into this abuse. Or, they have discovered it is going on.

8 Swords + 5 Pentacles + 7 Cups

An illness (bronchitis, asthma) with their lungs that is caused by smoking, fumes, dust, pollen. Or, the illness is causing poor oxygen exchange in their lungs.

8 Swords + Knight Swords (rev) + 5 Cups

A grievous situation because it is lung cancer. Or, they grieve over someone who was trapped or kidnapped but not rescued.

8 Swords (rev) + Sun + 2 Wands

Feeling free and uninhibited (unfettered) and looking forward with eager anticipation to their future and new goals. Or, are feeling free after being released from jail or a restricting situation.

8 Swords (rev) + 10 Cups + 5 Cups (rev)

Feeling no commitment to the family whatsoever (no regrets). Or, are free from the family and whatever agony this was causing.

9 Swords + Page Cups + Ace Cups (rev)

The child is crying because they feel they have been abandoned or they feel (or actually are) alone or feel they are unloved.

9 Swords + 6 Wands + Page Pentacles

The sorrow of a sad story brings recognition (maybe even fame) and others give gifts, contributions, or donations to their cause.

9 Swords (rev) + Death + 4 Pentacles (rev)

All is forgiven. There is an end to their hurt feelings and they have let it go (not holding onto it anymore).

9 Swords (rev) + 8 Wands + 10 Wands

They have stopped crying or feeling sorry for themselves quite suddenly (that's it!) and are getting down to the work at hand (moving on).

10 Swords + 10 Wands + Chariot

A pedestrian, who is walking or jogging, is hit by a car. Or, successfully taking control over a devastating situation with hard work.

10 Swords + 6 Pentacles + 6 Cups

They are being financially drained by the children. Or, they are financially helping bring the kids out of a devastating situation.

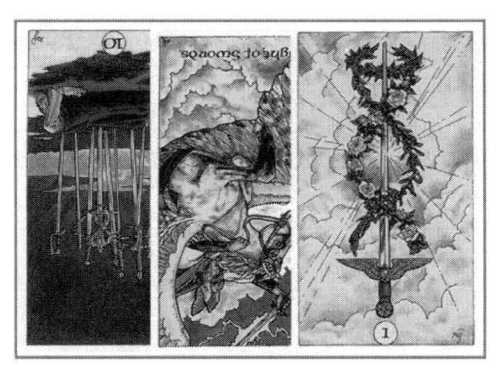

10 Swords (rev) + Knight Swords (rev) + Ace Swords

Resentment and anger that they feel is righteous and that they are fighting the good fight. Resentment and anger that leads to a kind of war.

10 Swords (rev) + Page Pentacles + Queen Pentacles

They resent that they have to give child support or some other payment to this woman.

Page Swords + 8 Swords + Justice

Urgent news that someone is in jail and caught up in the legal system. Or, they are going to court, needing a bail bondsman or an attorney.

Page Swords + World + Tower

Urgent news from overseas or out of state about a disaster (could be weather related like floods, fires, earthquakes). Or, hearing about a plane and a disaster. This is what 911 looked like (plus ace of swords).

Page Swords (rev) + 9 Cups (rev) + 10 Pentacles

Not happy with an unruly out of control child with behavioral issues being in the home. If not their child, then they don't like it when this child comes to their home.

Page Swords (rev) + 6 Cups + Ace Pentacles (rev)

A gang of kids are vandalizing and causing property damage (ace pentacles rev).

Knight swords + 2 Pentacles + World (rev)

They repeatedly come to the rescue or go get them and bring them back (like a yo-yo) and there never seems to be any end to this cycle.

Knight Swords + Queen Swords + Hanged Man

An ambulance takes them to the hospital (queen swords) and they are possibly put on life support (hanged man) because their life hangs in the balance.

Knight Swords (rev) + Lovers + Ace Wands (rev)

Cancer of the reproductive organs or sexual organs and having chemotherapy or radiation (ace wands). Or, the cancer is a sexually transmittable virus (like HPV).

Knight Swords (rev) + Devil + 3 Cups

Cancer caused by toxins in the food (like aspartame). Or, poisoned the food out of anger. Or, they are angry about the spoiled and rotten food.

Queen Swords + Magician + Ace Cups

A nurse or healer who is very skilled in their craft and they have a passion for humanity and what they do.

Queen Swords + Star + Hierophant

This woman is an alien abductee. Star card could mean the new-age term of "star-child" or "star-seed" and hierophant being "alien", of a different culture or tradition. Or, her carrier is different or eccentric.

Queen Wands (rev) + 9 Wands + 9 Cups (rev)

Their feelings were hurt so they are on the defensive and are being unfriendly.

Queen Wands (rev) + 6 Cups + 2 Wands (rev)

Sharp tongued, hurtful person from childhood that damaged their self-esteem and sense of confidence. Or, someone is doing this to a child now.

King Swords + World + 4 Swords

A soldier flies back for some R&R, meaning for some rest and relaxation. Soldier flies home for a vacation and time off.

King Swords + Hierophant (rev) + King Wands

This is a homosexual couple. Possibly, though less so, they are two foreigner males.

King Swords (rev) + 8 Pentacles + Ace Swords (rev)

Neurotic male plotting and planning to perpetuate a harmful act. Ace of swords rev is war, gun, or knife. (Ace of wands is gun, explosions, fire).

King Swords (rev) + Death + 3 Swords

A dangerous neurotic male who has killed before and will kill again. Or, they completely ended and severed their connection with this neurotic male; could have divorced them.

Cups

Ace Cups + 4 Cups + Queen Cups

They really love their mother (or wife) but are disappointed in her at the same time.

Ace Cups + Page Wands + 2 Pentacles (rev)

Communicating or proclaiming their love but it isn't being returned in kind. One loves the other but it isn't being reciprocated.

Ace Cups (rev) + 6 Swords + 4 Swords

They took the trip alone and they are sleeping alone. Could also read that they left because they don't love them anymore and they are at peace with this.

Ace Cups (rev) + 4 Wands (rev) + 5 Cups

They grieve because there is no love in their marriage. Or, they grieve because they never fell in love and haven't married. Doesn't mean they won't ever.

2 Cups + Death + 8 Wands

A relationship, friendship, or agreement that is on again and off again. Stop. Go. Stop. Go.

2 Cups + King Wands + 8 Cups

An agreement with this male for one or the other to walk away. Agreeing to cut ties with something or each other.

2 Cups (rev) + 2 Swords (rev) + Hierophant (rev)

A stalemate. Can't come to an agreement regarding a decision to be made due to religious, cultural, or ethical differences, or other prejudices.

2 Cups (rev) + Hanged Man + 8 Swords

A disagreement has put things in limbo and they are being prohibited from doing anything without that.

3 Cups + Judgement + 3 Pentacles

They work at a club or restaurant where women are on exhibit (like Hooters) or naked (strip clubs). Or, they work at a place where women or others exercise (like Curves).

3 Cups + Ace Swords (rev) + 10 Cups (rev)

Big fight in the family over food. Maybe someone is eating all the food or they aren't buying any. Or, this is a big drunken family fight.

3 Cups (rev) + Blank + Moon

A drunken blackout where they don't remember what they did. The moon card represents the effects on the brain due to alcoholic amnesia. *If they pass out drunk, or vomit, it indicates alcohol poisoning.

3 Cups (rev) + 5 Pentacles + Death (rev)

They have had diabetes a long time and are ill because of it and might even have an amputation. Reversed death means chronic. Or, chronic illness due to alcohol (ex: cirrhosis of liver).

4 Cups + King Cups + Knight Pentacles (rev)

They are disappointed in their husband (or father) because they aren't helping out financially and don't help or support them.

4 Cups + 8 Pentacles + Page Cups

Disappointed in child's performance at school (bad report card). Or, disappointed in what the child wrote. Or, child writes of disappointment in a letter or a diary. Or, not happy with what they read about this child.

4 Cups (rev) + Strength + Page Pentacle

Pet or other animal being focused and motivated (trained) by being rewarded with treats or toys (gifts).

4 Cups (rev) + 2 Cups + 9 Cups

Disappointment has turned to an agreement that they are happy about.

5 Cups + Queen Cups (rev) + Hermit

A beautiful woman is grieving over the loss of her youthful appearance due to getting older. Or, they are grieving the loss of their mother or wife and are looking for her. Or, they are looking for their birth mother.

5 Cups + Strength + Ace Wands

They are grieving over the loss of a pet but the animal is still alive. This is good news if the animal got lost or was stolen.

5 Cups (rev) + Ace Cups + Fool

They are no longer grieving over a prior loss and are embarking on a new love.

5 Cups (rev) + Hermit + 4 Swords

They got over their grief with counseling or therapy and are enjoying peace of mind.

6 Cups + 7 Cups + 9 Swords

Childhood nightmares or night terrors. Or, the kids cry because of scary imagery; pictures, movies, or violent video games. Or, crying because they imagine things about the kids that might not be real.

6 Cups + High Priestess + 8 Cups

They have left the secrets of their childhood, or information of a personal nature, behind them.

6 Cups (rev) + 4 Wands + Star (rev)

This couple does not have children but they want kids so their hopes and dreams are not being fulfilled.

6 Cups (rev) + Chariot + Justice

Problems with kids and vehicles and the legal system; tickets, loss of driver's license, no insurance, joy rides, vandalized vehicles.

7 Cups + Lovers + Page Wands

Sexual images being broadcast. Porn sites. Phone sex. Posting or receiving illicit images on the webcam, cell phone or partaking in things of a sexual nature on Skype.

7 Cups + 6 Wands (rev) + Justice (rev)

A misunderstanding or misperception is hurting their reputation and they are being misjudged, or are having legal problems because of it.

7 Cups (rev) + 10 Pentacles + Strength (rev)

An odor or some kind of chemicals in the house is bothering the pet (carpet freshener, polishes, sprays, cigarette smoke). Or, the house has pet odors.

7 Cups (rev) + 9 Wands + 4 Pentacles

They are defending their heavy smoking and don't plan on giving it up. They don't want to quit and will argue and not back down.

8 Cups + 6 Swords + 2 Cups

Leaving everything else behind in order to pursue an agreement or partnership elsewhere.

8 Cups + 10 Pentacles + Ace Wands

They left the house and it caught on fire. They weren't there when the building caught on fire or the explosion happened.

8 Cups (rev) + Strength (rev) + Ace Cups (rev)

They don't leave because they are afraid to be alone, or are afraid no one will love them. Strength card can be upright or reversed and can still be read as being afraid.

8 Cups (rev) + Page Cups + Strength

The pet does not want to leave the child. Or, the child does not want to leave the pet. Or, they don't want to leave the pet because they see it as being their child.

9 Cups + Knight Pentacles + Hermit

They are very happy to help out either financially and with guidance or supervision. Happy to help.

9 Cups + King Wands (rev) + 2 Cups

Remaining on good terms with the ex-husband or ex-boyfriend. Or, this obnoxious male is friendly with and only likes them, for some reason.

9 Cups (rev) + Knight Wands + Fool

They are unhappy and want to move and start over somewhere else; getting a fresh start.

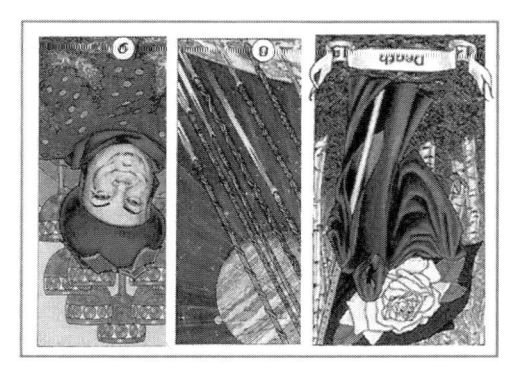

9 Cups (rev) + 8 Wands (rev) + Death (rev)

They have been unhappy for a very, very long time. The situation is in a stagnant holding pattern. They need to refresh their life.

10 Cups + 3 Cups + World

A family celebration or family reunion where everyone comes together. It is taking place out of state, or even overseas.

10 Cups + 7 Cups + 9 Cups

Happy pictures of the family. Remembering the family fondly. Or, giving a false impression that the family is happy or they are happy with their family.

10 Cups (rev) + Ace Swords (rev) + Strength

Big family fight over the animal(s) (domestic or non-domestic; and includes horses or cattle). Or, they are acting as the peacemaker and mediator for a feuding family.

10 Cups (rev) + 10 Pentacles + Knight Wands (rev)

The family is being evicted out of the house; being forced to move. Or, the family throws them out of the house.

Page Cups + 7 Pentacles + 8 Pentacles

This precocious child is both working and going to school or is in training for the job.

Page Cups + Ace Cups + Hierophant

They love this child very much but there is something different or eccentric about them. Or, the beloved child is of a different race or they are gay.

Page Cups (rev) + 9 Wands + Devil

A stubborn and defiant problem-child who is doing drugs.

Page Cups (rev) + Empress (rev) + 4 Pentacles

Smothering mother who is clinging to a disabled child in an overly protective way. Could suggest that she is stunting the child's development by her behavior.

Knight Cups + Page Pentacles + High Priestess

A suitor gave them a gift(s) that they are keeping secret. Or, an opportunity to make some money that they are keeping confidential.

Knight Cups + 6 Swords + Sun

Opportunity to take a trip to a sunny location or to the beach. Could be a cruise or boating. Looks like a vacation opportunity.

Knight Cups (rev) + Empress + Queen Wands

One of these two women is being cheated on. If Empress is their wife, then they are cheating with a fire sign. If wife is the fire sign, then they have someone pregnant.

Knight Cups (rev) + Star (rev) + 9 Swords

Loss of their romantic relationship has crushed their hopes and dreams and they are crying over it. The breakup.

Queen Cups + Tower + 6 Wands

This woman (water sign, wife, mother) receives recognition during a disaster. She is a heroine. Note the effects positive cards have when they flank a negative card.

Queen Cups + 2 Swords + 6 Cups

Wife or mother is having to choose sides with the kids. They could be having a dispute. Or, wife is being asked to make a choice between someone or something and the kids. Or, having to choose between their (new) wife and their kids.

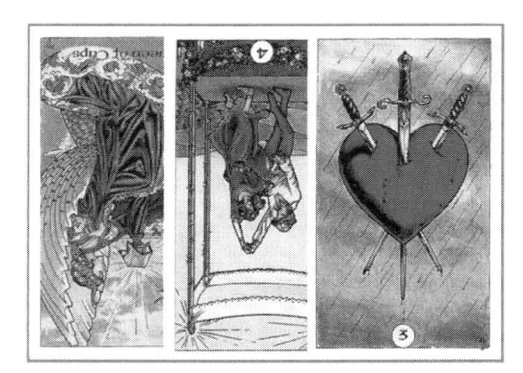

Queen Cups (rev) + 4 Wands (rev) + 3 Swords

The wife wants a divorce. Or, a problem with the wife has caused the divorce.

Queen Cups (rev) + High Priestess (rev) + Chariot

A gossiping and untrustworthy woman is revealing confidential information to gain control and to direct a situation.

King Cups + 6 Pentacles + 2 Wands

Their dad believes in them and is helping them with their goals for their future. He is backing them.

King Cups + Page Pentacles + Page Cups

This father has two children; one is not biological (page pentacles) and the other is theirs (page cups). Or, page of pentacles show this father is paying child support.

King Cups (rev) + 5 Swords + Lovers

Husband is cheating. Lovers card can be upright or reversed in this type of combination and could have a 7 swords in place of 5 swords.

King Cups (rev) + 7 Cups + Queen Wands (rev)

A misunderstanding and fall out with their dad (or their husband) and one or the other has withdrawn contact and is not talking to them.

WANDS

Ace Wands + Page Cups + Hermit (rev)

This child is alive but those concerned don't know where they are and they can't find them.

Ace Wands + 3 Cups + 9 Pentacles

Feeling alive and living life to the fullest (celebrating life) in a safe and secure environment. A safe haven for a group of pregnant women.

Ace Wands (rev) + 10 Pentacles + Tower

A disastrous house fire, or some other building fire, could even be a fire in the bedroom, apartment, hotel.

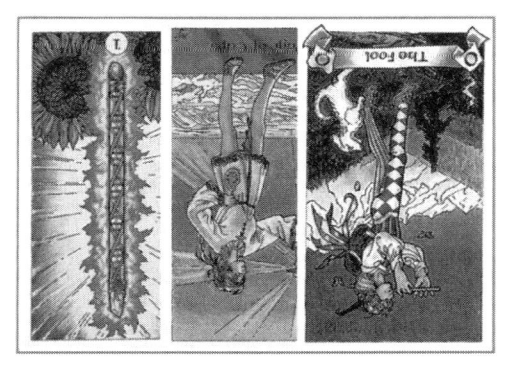

Ace Wands (rev) + Page Cups (rev) + Fool (rev)

These three cards each indicate a handicapped person: genetic defect; disability; and mentally slow with low IQ. Or, this foolish troublesome child set a fire or explosion.

2 Wands + 8 Wands + 9 Pentacles

They are looking forward to good prospects on the horizon that promises advances and brings financial security.

2 Wands + 8 Pentacles + 10 Cups

Having good self-esteem both in school and in their home. Well adjusted, self-confident in both school and with their family.

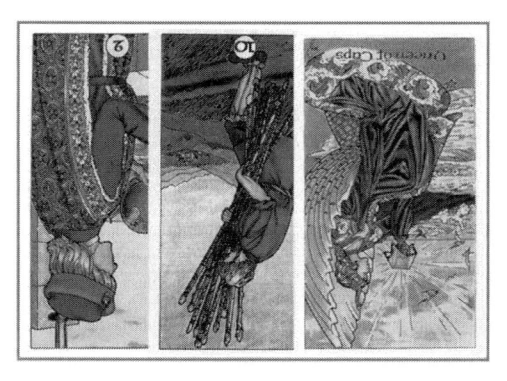

2 Wands (rev) + 10 Wands (rev) + Queen Cups (rev)

Low self-esteem due to weight (too heavy or too thin) and feels ugly. Or, low self-esteem causing them to not take on the responsibility of being a good mother; maybe they don't think they can be.

2 Wands (rev) + 5 Swords + Page Wands (rev)

Low self-esteem due to someone saying cruel things. Or, they pick on others because of their own low self-esteem.

3 Wands + 2 Cups + Ace Pentacles

A business partnership that brings them a lot of money. Or, they both invest a significant sum of money into the business. This partnership looks fair and equitable.

3 Wands + 10 Cups + 7 Wands

A family business that is successful. This doesn't guarantee long term success because we are only looking at a moment in time. Remember, you can specify a time frame.

3 Wands (rev) + Death + 4 Cups

The business has come to an end or closed and they are disappointed about this. Could be their business or even a business that they liked and now it is gone.

3 Wands (rev) + Page Pentacles + King Pentacles

Business isn't doing so well but they are able to make loan payments to the bank, or they have something left over to deposit in the bank.

4 Wands + 6 Swords + 3 Cups

A wedding that includes a honeymoon cruise or celebration on a boat. Or, the wedding celebration takes place elsewhere so that they travel to the wedding or party.

4 Wands + 2 Swords + Moon

There is mental strain in making a decision regarding getting married. It's like asking, why-why-why, or how-how-how.

4 Wands (rev) + 3 Swords + Empress

Divorced or separated and the wife or ex-wife is pregnant. Or, because their marriage failed, she got an abortion.

4 Wands (rev) + Hermit + 8 Cups (rev)

Marriage problems for which they go to counseling so that they don't walk away from their relationship.

5 Wands + Hermit + 7 Cups

Worried that something is going to come to light or be found out where their intentions could be misunderstood.

5 Wands + 4 Pentacles + Strength

Worried about being able to keep the pet or other animal. Worried about having possession of an animal, maybe one they shouldn't have, is considered dangerous, or is not on the lease.

5 Wands (rev) + 7 Swords + Fool

They aren't worried about criminal activity (but it is obviously there) and they walk right into it. Showing no concern and being very naïve about a criminal person in their presence.

5 Wands (rev) + Strength + Page Wands

Communicating a message that is meant to relieve worry and bring encouragement. A motivational speaker; "don't worry, be happy".

6 Wands + Emperor + 10 Cups

There is a famous leader in their family, probably holding legal or political office. Or, they receive recognition because of their familial relationship with this powerful person (nepotism).

6 Wands + Queen Wands + Judgement

A famous woman who receives recognition for her performance abilities which requires use of her body (gymnastics, runner, dancer, skater, swimmer, tennis, stripper).

6 Wands (rev) + Knight Swords (rev) + 5 Swords

They are angry about being disrespected (loss of honor) and they plan to get their revenge. They will want to get back at them for it.

6 Wands (rev) + Devil + Page Wands

Someone is talking "smack" on them. Communicating things meant to ruin their reputation and air their dirty laundry.

7 Wands + World + 4 Swords

Successful completion of something from which they are taking a break, getting some much need rest.

7 Wands + High Priestess + Justice

They successfully presented all the information they needed to win this case. They get the upper hand with information that would otherwise have been confidential.

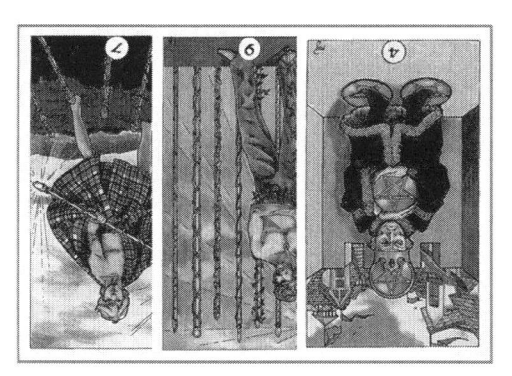

7 Wands (rev) + 9 Wands (rev) + 4 Pentacles (rev)

They failed and aren't going to pursue it any longer. They have given up and have just let it go.

7 Wands (rev) + 2 Cups (rev) + 4 Cups

Unable to come to an agreement and being disappointed about it.

8 Wands + Lovers + 4 Wands

A whirlwind relationship that quickly advances to marriage.

8 Wands + Ace Swords + Wheel of Fortune

Advances in techniques or technology is very fortunate for them. Example: cataract surgery is relatively new without which they would have gone blind.

8 Wands (rev) + 6 Swords + 8 Cups

Delayed their trip and when they got there the other person was already gone. Or, trip was being delayed but they go anyway leaving something un-finished behind.

8 Wands (rev) + Ace Pentacles (rev) + 5 Wands

There is loss of progress and loss of a large amount of money and profit and this brings worry and concerns.

9 Wands + Temperance + Judgement

By taking a stand and not backing down, in due time with proper handling and patience they will succeed and come through this very well.

9 Wands + Ace Cups + Page Wands

Declaring they will defend and love that person. Speaking up in a defensive manner for someone they love.

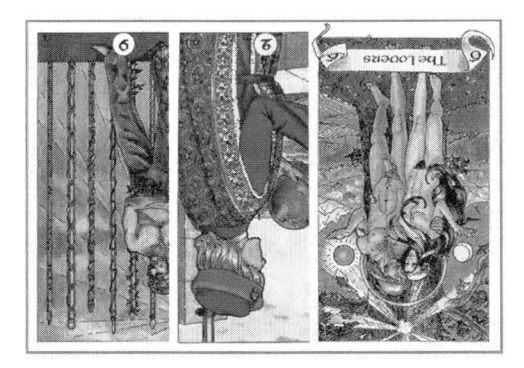

9 Wands (rev) + 2 Wands (rev) + Lovers (rev)

They lack backbone and self-esteem and this leads to them being mistreated in relationships or to not establishing a good relationship.

9 Wands (rev) + 2 Swords + 4 Swords

They or someone else chooses to give up their position. This brings peace of mind. Maybe it is not worth it anymore to continue this battle.

10 Wands + Page Pentacles + King Pentacles

Working hard to "squirrel it away" and creating a nest egg. Working hard and making deposits into a savings or retirement account.

10 Wands + 3 Pentacles + Temperance (rev)

They are taking on a heavy load of more responsibilities at work and this is causing a lot of stress and feeling run-down. Stress puts one's energy off balance.

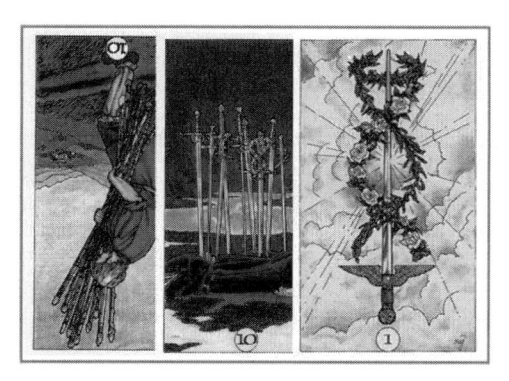

10 Wands (rev) + 10 Swords + Ace Swords

Difficulty walking due to back problems that is causing a lot of sharp, stabbing pains (ace swords).

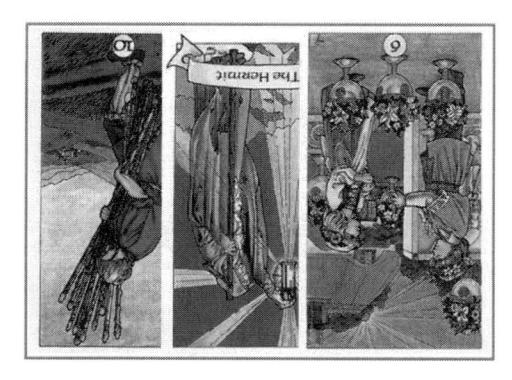

10 Wands (rev) + Hermit (rev) + 6 Cups (rev)

No one is taking responsibility for or supervising the children. This is causing problems for the kids who are being neglected or these kids are causing problems because of it.

Page Wands + 2 Swords + 6 Swords

Something communicated that is a deciding factor that causes them to either leave a situation or go towards a situation.

Page Wands + Queen Swords (rev) + Hermit

They are talking about their old hurts and unhealed wounds to a therapist or counselor.

Page Wands (rev) + Tower + 8 Cups

Communications cut off due to a disaster, probably weather related. And because of the disaster, they have been displaced and are moving (refugees, evacuees, migrants).

Page Wands (rev) + Fool + 7 Cups

Not being told or notified of something and going on in ignorance of it and laboring under a misunderstanding or under a misperception.

Knight Wands + World + 10 Pentacles

Moving overseas, or to another state, to another house.

Knight Wands + 8 Swords + King Wands (rev)

Their ex-boyfriend or ex-husband has forced them to another location (basically kidnapping them). Or, an obnoxious male (possibly an ex) is taken to jail.

Knight Wands (rev) + 4 Swords + Chariot

They were evicted, forced to move, and are now sleeping in their vehicle.

Knight Wands (rev) + 10 Wands (rev) + 5 Pentacles

Muscular disability (like MS or other neuromuscular diseases) or injured muscles or tendons causes them difficulty in walking. Tendonitis?

Queen Wands + 8 Wands + 6 Swords

This fire-sign (blond or red haired) woman is going to take a sudden unexpected trip.

Queen Wands + Death + Knight Cups

This woman is seen as blocking their opportunity. Or, an offer is being blocked from her. From a reading where she wouldn't loan them money to pursue something.

Queen Wands (rev) + Empress (rev) + 6 Cups

Avoiding (withdrawn from) their "smothering-mother". From a reading for an overbearing mother where her son won't answer her phone calls.

Queen Wands (rev) + 5 Pentacles + King Cups (rev)

A woman (or any person) is shut-down, reserved, due to abuse by either her father or her husband. Or, communication has been cut off because of the abuse from this man.

King Wands + Knight Cups+ Lovers

They are involved in a romantic and sexual relationship with a fire-sign male (or, he has blond or red hair or it is a gay relationship).

King Wands + 2 Swords + King Swords

These two men are involved in a decision. Could be that they are on opposite sides and may be split in their opinion. Look for other indicators if they finally agree.

King Wands (rev) + 2 Cups (rev) + 4 Pentacles

Trying to break off with an obstinate ex (boyfriend or friend) but he doesn't want to let go. Or, this arrogant male won't agree to share.

King Wands (rev) + 3 Cups (rev) + 7 Pentacles

A loud, or belligerent male who is drunk or drinking on the job.

Pentacles

Ace Pentacles + 8 Pentacles + 8 Wands

A significant sum of money towards advancement in education. Could be towards a student, a classroom or a school.

Ace Pentacles + 2 Pentacles + Hierophant

The wiring and transfer of a large amount of money to a foreign country, or maybe wiring to a religious organization. The Vatican bank. Could be money laundering.

Ace Pentacles (rev) + 4 Wands (rev) + 9 Swords

The loss of a large amount of money is causing marital problems and one or both are upset and possibly even crying about it. Financial problems cause marriage problems.

Ace Pentacles (rev) + World (rev) + Tower

Mechanical failure (rev ace pents) causes something to fall from the sky (air plane, satellite, space shuttle, drone). Of course, this is a disaster.

2 Pentacles + 2 Cups + Page Pentacles

An agreement for an exchange of items (2 pents) for a fee or payment (page pent). Or, friends exchange gifts (page pents).

2 Pentacles + Knight Cups + 4 Wands

Deliberating whether to pursue the romance to become partners or to get engaged with intent to marry.

2 Pentacles (rev) + 9 Swords + King Swords

They fell and got hurt bad enough that they have to see a surgeon.

2 Pentacles (rev) + 3 Pentacles + 8 Pentacles

Difficulty in juggling both work and school.

3 Pentacles + 6 Pentacles + 7 Pentacles

Working two jobs to make ends meet and pay all the bills. Or, working two jobs because they are giving money to help someone else.

3 Pentacles + Hermit + 8 Wands

Someone at work is watching them or "checking them out" for advancement or promotion. They are under consideration to move up in the company.

3 Pentacles (rev) + 3 Swords + 6 Wands (rev)

Either quit their job or were fired (3 swords) and feel they have been dishonored, disrespected and unappreciated (6 wands rev).

3 Pentacles (rev) + Queen Cups (rev) + Ace Swords (rev)

A horrible job where there is gossip (men or women) and environment is hostile and critical. They need to consider finding a different job.

4 Pentacles + 4 Wands (rev) + Justice

A dispute over possession or greed has entered into the divorce and will have to be disputed with their divorce attorney or in the courts.

4 Pentacles + 9 Wands + 5 Swords

Hanging on to it and will not back down. This is causing difficulties. Or, they are hanging on in a vindictive manner with ill intent (spite) and don't care about the harm done.

4 Pentacles (rev) + Knight Swords (rev) + 2 Cups (rev)

They are letting go of their claim to something but are very angry about it and are breaking any relationship or friendship that was there.

4 Pentacles (rev) + Page Wands + Ace Cups

A forgiving going on where they let it go and express love. "I forgive you because I love you". Or, they give over a possession and express love.

5 Pentacles + 3 Cups + 9 Wands

From a reading where client had suffered poverty and alcoholic parents in childhood. He didn't want that in his life anymore and was taking a stand against it.

5 Pentacles + Justice + Page Pentacles

Certified illness (disability) for which they get payment. Courts or other legal obligation to pay for illness or injury caused.

5 Pentacles (rev) + 8 Wands + Judgement

An illness that improves very quickly (8 wands) to full recovery (judgement).

5 Pentacles (rev) + 3 Cups + 4 Swords

Illness is improving and they are eating and sleeping better. Or, proper food and rest are helping them to recover.

6 Pentacles + King Wands + 6 Swords

Giving money to this fellow so that he can either take a trip or to help him out of his troubles (hot water).

6 Pentacles + Page Swords + Tower

Helping out due to urgent news of a disaster.

6 Pentacles (rev) + 10 Wands + 4 Swords (rev)

Difficulty making ends meet and paying all the bills so they are working hard and losing sleep.

6 Pentacles (rev) + 5 Wands + 6 Cups

Worried about not having enough money for the kid's needs. Or, worried about their siblings or "the kids" not having enough money.

7 Pentacles + Fool + Page Cups

A young person has entered the work force and started their very first job. They are a "newbie".

7 Pentacles + 8 Swords + 10 Wands

Feeling trapped in a hard job. A prison worker doing menial labor. Forced to do labor (labor camp, sweat shop, work release program).

7 Pentacles (rev) + 7 Wands (rev) + Moon

Not successful at their job, or even losing their job, due to mental issues; being forgetful, poor comprehension.

7 Pentacles (rev) + 8 Cups + 5 Wands

They walked off their job or just didn't show up and now they are worried about it. Worried about having gone AWOL from work.

8 Pentacles + Knight Wands + Hermit

Student travels or moves to seek instruction of a higher learning (college) or to do research.

8 Pentacles + 3 Cups + 6 Wands

A graduation ceremony. Could be that they receive honors or other recognition at this graduation.

8 Pentacles (rev) + 3 Swords + 5 Swords

Quit school or really hates school because they are being bullied and picked on. Or, quit because they find it too difficult and problematic.

8 Pentacles (rev) + Justice (rev) + Death

Failed the exam or test and that is the end of it because they can't move on from there. This exam was their last chance. Being permanently expelled from school.

9 Pentacles + Strength + 5 Pentacles

A rescue shelter (farm or zoo) for homeless, sick, or abused animals. Or, an outdoor pet or animal is diseased or injured.

9 Pentacles + 10 Pentacles + Page Wands

Buying (or selling) a luxurious home in an affluent neighborhood or gated community. Or, buying (or selling) furnishings for the home.

9 Pentacles (rev) + Hermit + Knight Swords

An unsafe (depressed) environment where lighting or surveillance has been added, along with a police presence.

9 Pentacles (rev) + 6 Swords + 2 Wands

Lack of financial security has them leaving for greener pastures and seeking a better future. Prospects are looking better elsewhere.

10 Pentacles + Page Wands + 7 Wands

They successfully buy or sale this house.

10 Pentacles + Hanged man + Death (rev)

House is haunted. There is at least one entity there but they don't think they are dead. Or, house has chronic, stubborn infestation of some biting or stinging insect, spiders, or snakes.

10 Pentacles (rev) + King Swords (rev) + 5 Swords

A neurotic and problematic male (neighbor, landlord) associated with this house or apartment. If question is whether to move there, then advise is against it (neighbor or landlord from hell).

10 Pentacles (rev) + 5 Wands (rev) + 8 Cups

Having issues with the house or property and decide that it would be best to walk away than to worry about it all the time.

Page Pentacles + 4 Pentacles (rev) + 6 Wands (rev)

A gift (or money) that was not kept or wanted and the rejection is meant or perceived as an insult or show of disrespect.

Page Pentacles + 3 Cups + 6 Cups

Payments to feed the kids, this could be food stamps or meal tickets for school lunches. Or, gifts or paying for a children's party celebration.

Page Pentacles (rev) + Chariot + 2 Swords (rev)

Not making the car payment or repair is a poor decision. They will regret the decision of not making that car payment or car repair.

Page Pentacles (rev) + 6 Swords (rev) + 4 Cups

No money for the ticket or fee means they don't get to take the trip and they are very disappointed and sulking about it.

Knight Pentacles+ 10 Pentacles + Judgement

Getting the money to do renovations, restoration and repairs on the house. Could be an escrow loan on the house.

Knight Pentacles + 5 Swords + 6 Pentacles (rev)

Lying about what they are going to do with the money. They aren't going to pay those bills, or they aren't going to give you any of it.

Knight Pentacles (rev) + 3 Swords + Empress

Elder woman cuts them off financially (cut purse strings) or she is the one cut off financially. Or, they really hate (3 swords) her for cutting them off financially.

Knight Pentacles (rev) + Hermit (rev) + Strength (rev)

They have lost money, a check, or a credit card. They can't find it and this is very scary.

Queen Pentacles + Emperor (rev) + 3 Wands

A woman who manages her business very well but is demanding and controlling. These ruthless, hardline tactics may be key to her success.

Queen Pentacles + Ace Swords + 9 Cups

This woman is seen has having a very positive (ace swords) and friendly (9 cups) personality. She might be an earth sign, dark skinned, or work in banking.

Queen Pentacles (rev) + Page Wands + 9 Pentacles

Financially broke because they are always buying luxury items. Beer pocketbook with champagne tastes. Or, selling something (or speaking) reverses their financial situation.

Queen Pentacles (rev) + Hierophant + 7 Cups (rev)

A dark skinned foreign woman is imagining things. She has a poor sense of reality or grasp of what is really the truth of the matter.

King Pentacles + Hermit + Wheel of Fortune

Inheriting a large amount of money from an elder (hermit). Or, discovering (hermit) a large amount of money somewhere.

King Pentacles + Knight Wands + Page Pentacles (rev)

They are moving away and taking the savings with them and they are not going to leave or share any of it.

King Pentacles (rev) + Wheel of Fortune (rev) + 10 Swords

Huge loss of money that is an unfortunate turn of events that devastates them. Bankruptcy (completely wiped out).

King Pentacles (rev) + 7 Cups + Death

Major loss of money with a smoke screen blocking the pursuit of it or where it went. This is how the bank bailout scandal of 2008 looked.

Medical Assignments

Some cards have a medical issue assigned to them. You can also assign your own if you like. Just remember that you cannot diagnose or give medical advice without a medical license. At the same time, if used judiciously, you just might save a life.

3 Empress ~ Pregnancy. Abdominal issues, which includes stomach, uterus and ovaries or the breasts, gallbladder, pancreas.

6 Lovers ~ Reproductive organs, which includes private areas. For men, it is prostate issues. Also indicates all transmittable diseases and infections from person to person and not just those that are sexually transmitted (example: MRSA).

8 Strength ~ Allergies. Bacteria. Parasites. Anxiety disorders. Panic attacks. Chronic fatigue.

9 Hermit ~ Vision problems. Cataracts. Blind. Elderly. Any person or object that is old (ex: old food, old clothes, old car, old house). Decrepit. Senior.

11 Justice ~ Medical tests and diagnostics.

12 Hanged Man ~ Head and neck areas. Choked. Drowned. Hanged. Beheaded. Suffocated. Strangled. A disincarnate entity. A spirit attachment or influence. Snake, spider, scorpion, or other biting insects.

13 Death ~ Chronic condition. Menopause. In a dormant state. In remission.

14 Temperance ~ Stress. Burn out. Metals in the body (lead, aluminum).

15 Devil ~ Addictions. Toxins. Poison. Rotten. Pollutants.

18 Moon ~ Mental aberrations and illness. Confusion. ADHD. Schizophrenia. Bipolar. Stroke. Coma. Unconscious. Amnesia. Dementia. Alzheimer's. Hallucinations. Sun Downers (elderly who get more confused-agitated at night). Cysts. Growths. Tumors.

19 Sun ~ Overheated. Sun Stroke. Sun burned. Depression. Seasonal Affective Disorder (SAD), which just means they need to get more sun.

20 Judgement ~ If upright it means full recovery and good health. Exercise. Physically fit. Acupuncture. Chiropractor. The naked body. If reversed, means poor health, doesn't recover, a thing is not purified or cleansed, immune system down, feeling drained of their energy. Slow metabolism.

21 World ~ Circulation. Metastasized. Blood pressure problems.

Ace Pentacles ~ Physical abuse.

2 Pentacles ~ Tripping. Falling. Problem with leg, feet, ankles. Sprains.

4 Pentacle ~ Arthritis. Problems with hands, arms, elbows.

5 Pentacles ~ Illness. Poverty. Abuse. Abandoned. Neglect.

King Pentacles ~ The boss organ, which is the Liver. Cirrhosis. Hepatitis C. Liver Cancer. Pancreatic cancer or pancreatitis.

Ace of Cups ~ Pregnancy. Reversed is fluid overload. Congested heart failure (CHF).

2 Cups ~ Kidney problems.

3 Cups ~ Diabetic. Alcoholic. Food allergies. Malnutrition. Anorexia. Bulimia.

5 Cups ~ Blood loss. Anemia. Grief.

7 Cups ~ Smoke. Dust. Ash. Fumes. Odors. Heavy smoker. Carbon monoxide. Pollen. Pollution. Suffocation. Nightmares.

9 Cups ~ Unhappy. Bipolar. Emotionally unstable. Mood swings. Manic depressive. Goofy person.

Page Cups ~ Disabled, mentally or physically handicapped, mongoloid.

Knight Cups ~ Edema. Congestion.

Queen Cups ~ Cosmetic issues. Disfigured. Boils, warts, scars, acne, skin cancer.

King Cups ~ Doctor.

Ace Swords ~ Sharp pain. Needle stick. Shots. IV drug usage. IV therapy.

3 Swords ~ Accident or injury. Sudden illness. Death. Cut. Stabbed. Shot. Punctured. Ruptured. Surgery. Heart attack surgery. Pierces. Stroke. Tattoos.

4 Swords ~ Rest and relaxation. Bed rest. Sleep problems.

7 Swords ~ Crime being committed against them.

8 Swords ~ Lung or rib problems. Can't move.

9 Swords ~ Emotional or physical pain. Fibromyalgia.

10 Swords ~ Spinal problems. Broken back. Blood disorders. Ruptured Spleen. Metal plates or pins. Prosthetics. Exhaustion. Depleted.

Knight Swords ~ Cancer. Anger issues.

Queen Swords ~ Nurse. Clinic. Hospital. Healer.

King Swords ~ Surgeon (king cups = doctor)

Ace Wands ~ Pregnancy. Birth. Fertility. DNA. Sperm or Ova. Genetics. <u>Negative aspects:</u> Birth defects. Genetic or neurological disorders. Seizures. Fibromyalgia. Multiple Sclerosis. Chemical imbalances. Manic Depressive. Hormones. PMS. Sprains. Strains. Broken bone. Neutropenia. Leukemia, Allergies. Immuno-suppressed. Bacteria & viruses (flu, small pox, hepatitis, herpes, molds, fungus, AIDS). Chemotherapy. Radiation. Antibiotics. Shocked or electrocuted. Burned. Inflammation. Impotency. Low libido.

5 Wands ~ Worry. Anxiety. Over thinking a thing.

10 Wands ~ Difficulty walking. Walking stooped over. Hunch back. Walks with a limp. Back, hip or knee problems. Uses walker, cane, or special shoes. Osteoarthritis. Weight issues. They are a "carrier" of this disease.

Page Wands ~ Problems with speech, and sound. Receptive or expressive problems. Aphasia. Laryngitis. Deaf or mute.

Knight Wands ~ Muscle and neuromuscular issues. Tremors. Parkinson's. Muscle cramps. Multiple Sclerosis. Gillian Barre. Muscular Dystrophy. Myasthenia Gravis. ALS or Lou Gehrig's Disease.

Quiz- just for fun

1. A decision based upon a misunderstanding.
    a. Two Swords + 7 Cups
    b. 2 Cups + Moon
2. Skilled at their job.
    a. Magician + 3 Pentacles
    b. 7 Pentacles + 7 Wands
3. Showing confidence in school.
    a. 10 Pentacles + 5 Swords
    b. 2 Wands + 6 Pentacles
4. They are pregnant.
    a. Ace Wands
    b. Lovers
5. A card that means opportunity or an offer.
    a. Knight Pentacles
    b. Knight Cups
6. Your client gets the Star card as the outcome. You tell them that.
    a. They will achieve their wish
    b. They will have good luck
    c. They need to mediate.
    d. Someone will help them.
7. If you get the Empress card in the thinking position it means that they are pregnant.
    a. True
    b. False
8. Being reborn quickly.
    a. Chariot + Empress
    b. Judgement + 8 Wands
9. Worried and confused.
    a. 5 Wands + Fool
    b. 5 Wands + Moon
10. Soldier takes a flight.
    a. King Swords + World
    b. Knight Swords + 8 Wands
11. Meeting bad weather on a trip.
    a. Chariot+ Devil
    b. 6 Swords + Tower

12. The card that means virgin, fidelity, or innocent and pure.
    a. Fool
    b. Temperance
13. The metaphysical meaning of the High Priestess is...
    a. Someone is spilling secrets.
    b. Casting spells.
    c. She is the creative force in the universe.
14. In medical readings, the King of Pentacles is the liver.
    a. True
    b. False
15. A birthday gift.
    a. Sun + Page Pentacles.
    b. 3 Cups + 7 Cups
16. Two cards that mean work.
    a. 7 Wands + 3 Pentacles
    b. 7 Pentacles + 3 Pentacles.
17. The house is haunted.
    a. Death + Justice
    b. Hanged Man + 10 Pentacles.
18. Full recovery from an illness.
    a. 8 Wands + Sun
    b. 5 Pentacles + Judgement.
19. If you get this card you need to stop everything and focus on it.
    a. Death
    b. 3 Swords
20. Pick the correct statement.
    a. A new deck of cards works right away.
    b. The death card means death.
    c. It is best to use no reversed card definitions.
    d. Magician is masculine and the conscious & High Priestess is feminine and the subconscious.
21. The feminine and masculine cards are paired as energetic opposites throughout the 22 major arcane.
    a. True
    b. False
22. This card means different, foreigner, homosexual, or alien.
    a. Hierophant
    b. Lovers

23. Which statement is true?
    a. All cards have a medical issue assigned to it.
    b. Sometimes you should take the reversed meaning of an upright card.
    c. Stick to only the assigned meanings of the card.
    d. The history of tarot is well known.
24. The Queen of Swords can mean healer, nurse, clinic, or hospital.
    a. True
    b. False
25. Cheating lover.
    a. Knight Cups + 7 Swords
    b. 9 Swords + Lovers
26. Protective or possessive of the child.
    a. 4 Pentacles + Page Cups
    b. 7 Wands + 6 Pentacles
27. Died of drug overdose.
    a. 3 Cups + 5 Wands
    b. Devil + 3 Swords
28. Financial security and wealth.
    a. 9 Pentacles + King Pentacles
    b. Ace Pentacles + King Wands
29. Which card could represent the rise and fall of the Golden and Dark ages of mankind?
    a. Magician
    b. Temperance
    c. 2 Pentacles
    d. Wheel of Fortune
30. Which statements is correct?
    a. Sometimes you can get your answer in one reading.
    b. Tarot can give you names and dates.
31. If you don't understand a layout, you should immediately try again.
    a. True
    b. False
32. Pet has sharp pain.
    a. Knight Wands + 3 Swords
    b. Strength + Ace Swords
33. They might be diabetic, or something they ate made them sick.
    a. 3 Cups + 5 Pentacles.
    b. 5 Pentacles + Emperor

34. They have chronic poor health.
    a. Judgement reversed + death reversed
    b. Devil + 5 Cups
35. Weather or disaster causes evacuations.
    a. Tower + 8 Cups.
    b. Emperor + Chariot
36. It is good to know the metaphysical meanings of the major arcana because; pick two.
    a. You can impress your clients.
    b. It is the path to enlightenment.
    c. You need to be able to explain it to your clients.
    d. It expands your consciousness.
37. Any of these 5 cards might be present surrounding a death, but one card can stand alone.
    a. 9 Swords
    b. 5 Cups
    c. 10 Swords
    d. 3 Swords
    e. Tower
    f. Death
38. A stern father.
    a. King Cups + Justice
    b. King Cups + Emperor
39. Obsessed with a vehicle.
    a. Moon + 6 Swords
    b. Devil + Chariot
40. Announcing or being told that they have a wife and children.
    a. 2 Cups + 4 Wands + Page Swords
    b. Page Wands + Queen Cups + 6 Cups
41. Which card is a time indicator?
    a. 8 Wands
    b. 7 Wands
42. Successful legal case.
    a. Tower + 9 Pentacles
    b. 7 Wands + Justice
43. Not seeing or finding it.
    a. Hermit reversed + 4 Pentacles
        b. Hermit reversed + Blank

44. Divine intervention in a grievous situation.
    a. 5 Cups + Temperance
    b. Page Swords + Temperance
45. Choose the three cards that mean some form of transformation.
    a. Death
    b. Temperance
    c. 6 Cups
    d. 7 Cups
    e. Judgement
46. Which is not true of the Hanged Man?
    a. Activation of pineal gland and intuition.
    b. That of sacrifice for the greater good.
    c. A literal hanging.
    d. Ghosts.
    e. Swimming.
47. Which card would be masculine and mean will power?
    a. Chariot
    b. Strength
48. Well received and admired by the family.
    a. 6 Swords + 10 Pentacles.
    b. 10 Cups + 6 Wands
49. A binding agreement.
    a. 2 Cups + 8 Swords
    b. 2 Swords + 4 Pentacles
50. Disability payments.
    a. Fool + Page Pentacles
    b. Knight Pentacles + 5 Pentacles
51. The World card can mean; pick three.
    a. Completion of the Fool's journey.
    b. Getting off the reincarnational wheel.
    c. Making the ascension to heaven.
    d. Flying during the day.
52. If you suspect someone's spouse is cheating, you are ethically obligated to tell them.
    a. True
    b. False
53. Pornography.
    a. Lovers + 4 Wands
    b. Lovers + Page Wands (or 7 Cups)

54. Which two cards can represent a boy and a girl?
    a. Page Pentacles + Queen Cups
    b. Page Swords + Page Cups
    c. Page Wands + Page Swords
55. People can block you from reading them, while others are an open book?
    a. True
    b. False
56. Still friends with their ex.
    a. 2 Cups + King Wands
    b. 9 Cups+ Knight Swords
57. Rescuing the children.
    a. Page Cups + 8 Cups
    b. Knight Swords + 6 Cups
58. You can read on the past, present, and future because (pick two).
    a. Tarot is magic.
    b. It is all in the way you lay out the cards.
    c. All is one mind.
    d. It is your intention to do so.
59. Proposing marriage.
    a. Page Wands + 4 Wands
    b. Knight Swords + 2 Cups reversed
60. Metaphysically, the Magician card means…
    a. Drawing energy from the unseen infinite to create in the physical.
    b. Performing magic with illusions
61. A barking dog.
    a. Strength + Page Wands
    b. Strength + 3 Cups
62. Fall with injury to head or neck.
    a. 2 Pentacles + Hanged man
    b. World reversed + Tower
63. Giving advice or guidance to the younger or less experienced.
    a. Hermit + Fool
    b. Temperance + 6 Cups
64. You are ready to become an awesome tarot reader.
    a. True
    b. false
65. Pick the three cards which means you are happy to complete this test.
    a. 9 Cups + 4 Swords + World
    b. 9 Cups + Justice + World

Test Answer Key.

1. A
2. A
3. B
4. A
5. B
6. A
7. B
8. B
9. A
10. A
11. B
12. A
13. C
14. A
15. A
16. B
17. B
18. B
19. B
20. D
21. A
22. A
23. B
24. A
25. A
26. A
27. B
28. A
29. D
30. A
31. B
32. B
33. A
34. A
35. A
36. B & D
37. D
38. B
39. B
40. B
41. A
42. B
43. B
44. A
45. A, B, E
46. E
47. A
48. B
49. A
50. A
51. A, B, C
52. B
53. B
54. B
55. A
56. A
57. B
58. C & D
59. A
60. A
61. A
62. A
63. A
64. A
65. B

1

10 Cups, **13**, 87, 101, 155, 164, 173, 180, 186, 187, 190, 220

10 Pentacles, **14**, 57, 65, 69, 71, 76, 81, 84, 89, 99, 122, 123, 129, 133, 150, 153, 160, 162, 163, 167, 177, 178, 180, 185, 196, 207, 208, 210, 216, 217, 220

10 Swords, **13**, 87, 135, 166, 194, 212, 215, 219

10 Wands, **12**, 69, 71, 87, 107, 115, 126, 148, 157, 165, 166, 186, 194, 196, 204, 205, 215

2

2 Cups, **13**, 57, 58, 87, 93, 125, 139, 145, 150, 172, 174, 178, 179, 187, 191, 198, 200, 202, 214, 216, 219, 220, 221

2 Pentacles, **14**, 68, 78, 102, 121, 159, 168, 171, 199, 200, 214, 218, 221

2 Swords, **12**, 56, 65, 70, 79, 91, 95, 135, 138, 141, 145, 150, 156, 158, 172, 183, 188, 193, 195, 198, 209, 220

2 Wands, **12**, 62, 76, 102, 107, 122, 134, 143, 146, 152, 164, 169, 184, 186, 193, 207, 216

3

3 Cups, **13**, 64, 65, 68, 80, 91, 92, 94, 97, 104, 108, 122, 129, 130, 141, 149, 154, 160, 163, 168, 173, 180, 185, 188, 198, 203, 206, 209, 214, 217, 218, 221

3 Pentacles, **14**, 70, 75, 91, 92, 98, 122, 126, 134, 138, 145, 148, 154, 157, 173, 194, 200, 201, 216, 217

3 Swords, **13**, 62, 80, 96, 117, 133, 135, 146, 157, 159, 170, 183, 188, 201, 206, 210, 214, 217, 218, 219

3 Wands, **12**, 66, 77, 93, 108, 157, 187, 211

4

4 Cups, **13**, 73, 95, 111, 125, 131, 145, 147, 162, 171, 174, 187, 191, 209

4 Pentacles, **14**, 86, 103, 111, 121, 123, 146, 150, 155, 158, 161, 165, 177, 181, 189, 191, 198, 202, 209, 218, 219, 220

4 Swords, **13**, 81, 127, 128, 139, 149, 152, 155, 160, 170, 171, 175, 191, 193, 196, 203, 204, 214, 221

4 Wands, **12**, 82, 85, 93, 101, 109, 137, 147, 151, 171, 176, 183, 188, 192, 199, 200, 202, 219, 220, 221

5

5 Cups, **13**, 68, 96, 114, 137, 146, 151, 164, 171, 175, 214, 219, 220

5 Pentacles, **14**, 62, 89, 92, 94, 105, 109, 114, 123, 124, 129, 136, 140, 142, 148, 162, 164, 173, 196, 197, 203, 207, 214, 217, 218, 220

5 Swords, **13**, 76, 82, 97, 104, 114, 124, 128, 135, 136, 138, 140, 144, 150, 161, 184, 186, 190, 202, 206, 208, 210, 216

5 Wands, **12**, 59, 70, 74, 79, 110, 113, 134, 152, 162, 189, 192, 204, 205, 208, 215, 216, 218

6

6 Cups, **13**, 85, 95, 97, 100, 111, 127, 134, 136, 154, 159, 166, 167, 169, 176, 183, 194, 197, 204, 209, 219, 220, 221

6 Pentacles, **14**, 61, 125, 162, 166, 184, 201, 204, 210, 216, 218

6 Swords, **13**, 75, 83, 152, 153, 162, 171, 178, 182, 188, 192, 195, 197, 204, 207, 209, 216, 219, 220

6 Wands, **12**, 89, 104, 111, 128, 131, 139, 144, 165, 177, 183, 190, 201, 206, 209, 220

7

7 Cups, **13**, 55, 66, 74, 81, 88, 93, 98, 106, 139, 143, 151, 164, 176, 177, 180, 184, 189, 195, 211, 212, 214, 216, 217, 220

7 Pentacles, **14**, 57, 85, 111, 126, 138, 155, 156, 181, 198, 201, 205, 216, 217

7 Swords, **13**, 63, 65, 69, 83, 84, 108, 120, 125, 127, 140, 141, 152, 156, 162, 163, 189, 215, 218

7 Wands, **12**, 58, 112, 136, 145, 148, 158, 161, 187, 191, 205, 208, 216, 217, 218, 219

8

8 Cups, **13, 55, 56, 67, 82, 90, 99, 109, 143, 149, 156, 172, 176, 178, 188, 192, 195, 205, 208, 219, 221**

8 Pentacles, **14, 56, 61, 79, 96, 98, 100, 105, 111, 127, 136, 143, 153, 160, 170, 174, 181, 186, 199, 200, 206**

8 Swords, **13, 60, 67, 79, 85, 97, 103, 106, 117, 134, 140, 147, 159, 164, 167, 172, 196, 205, 215, 220**

8 Wands, **12, 66, 70, 73, 79, 85, 99, 107, 109, 113, 120, 157, 158, 165, 172, 179, 186, 192, 197, 199, 201, 203, 216, 217, 219**

9

9 Cups, **13, 62, 69, 86, 100, 107, 114, 116, 122, 134, 145, 147, 167, 169, 174, 179, 180, 211, 214, 221**

9 Pentacles, **14, 72, 84, 109, 110, 120, 128, 142, 151, 153, 163, 185, 186, 207, 211, 218, 219**

9 Swords, **13, 86, 123, 139, 154, 165, 176, 182, 199, 200, 215, 218, 219**

9 Wands, **12, 57, 60, 82, 101, 114, 145, 169, 177, 181, 191, 193, 202, 203**

A

Ace Cups, **13, 92, 112, 140, 143, 153, 155, 160, 165, 169, 171, 175, 178, 181, 193, 202**

Ace Pentacles, **14, 63, 106, 120, 135, 144, 167, 187, 192, 199, 214, 218**

Ace Swords, **12, 71, 78, 99, 118, 148, 157, 166, 170, 173, 180, 192, 194, 201, 211, 214, 218**

Ace Wands, **12, 59, 66, 72, 76, 77, 90, 105, 106, 118, 121, 140, 144, 147, 153, 154, 159, 168, 175, 178, 185, 215, 216**

B

Blank, **12, 27, 156, 173, 219**

C

Chariot, **11, 19, 63, 72, 84, 116, 121, 131, 141, 159, 161, 163, 166, 176, 183, 196, 209, 216, 219, 220**

D

Death, **11, 22, 29, 67, 68, 69, 77, 78, 80, 110, 137, 138, 146, 147, 148, 151, 154, 158, 165, 170, 172, 173, 179, 187, 197, 206, 208, 212, 213, 214, 217, 219, 220**

Devil, **11, 60, 63, 71, 81, 94, 100, 112, 134, 149, 168, 181, 190, 213, 216, 218, 219**

E

Emperor, **11, 60, 100, 103, 108, 135, 138, 190, 211, 218, 219**

Empress, **11, 59, 80, 90, 112, 137, 144, 151, 153, 160, 163, 181, 182, 188, 197, 210, 213, 216**

F

Fool, **11, 56, 127, 131, 134, 142, 143, 146, 148, 150, 158, 161, 163, 175, 179, 185, 189, 195, 205, 216, 217, 220, 221**

H

Hanged Man, **11, 137, 146, 162, 168, 172, 213, 217, 220**

Hermit, **11, 64, 65, 72, 88, 98, 126, 132, 136, 143, 152, 156, 159, 163, 175, 179, 185, 188, 189, 194, 195, 201, 206, 207, 210, 212, 213, 219, 221**

Hierophant, **11, 61, 90, 113, 119, 132, 139, 145, 169, 170, 172, 181, 199, 211, 217**

High Priestess, **11, 58, 117, 136, 158, 176, 182, 183, 191, 217**

J

Judgement, **12, 56, 76, 82, 112, 124, 137, 142, 154, 160, 173, 190, 193, 203, 210, 213, 216, 217, 219, 220**

Justice, 11, 21, 58, 67, 74, 88, 102, 130, 134, 135, 141, 145, 146, 167, 176, 177, 191, 202, 203, 206, 213, 217, 219, 221

K

King Cups, 14, 59, 75, 84, 105, 139, 174, 184, 197, 214, 219
King Pentacles, 14, 73, 115, 133, 187, 194, 212, 214, 218
King Swords, 13, 91, 95, 98, 133, 142, 152, 157, 170, 198, 200, 208, 215, 216
King Wands, 12, 119, 160, 170, 172, 179, 196, 198, 204, 218, 221
Knight Cups, 13, 96, 103, 117, 139, 146, 182, 197, 198, 200, 214, 216, 218
Knight Pentacles, 14, 119, 130, 131, 144, 153, 174, 179, 210, 216, 220
Knight Swords, 13, 89, 106, 110, 119, 144, 150, 156, 159, 161, 162, 164, 166, 168, 190, 202, 207, 215, 216, 221
Knight Wands, 12, 83, 105, 117, 124, 147, 179, 180, 196, 206, 212, 215, 218

L

Lovers, 11, 27, 62, 78, 84, 93, 97, 101, 115, 138, 140, 149, 168, 177, 184, 192, 193, 198, 213, 216, 217, 218, 220

M

Magician, 11, 17, 57, 135, 152, 154, 169, 216, 217, 218, 221
Moon, 12, 74, 83, 89, 124, 126, 132, 142, 146, 152, 161, 173, 188, 205, 213, 216, 219

P

Page Cups, 13, 92, 102, 119, 141, 142, 156, 165, 174, 178, 181, 184, 185, 205, 214, 218, 221
Page Pentacles, 14, 75, 80, 130, 155, 156, 161, 166, 182, 184, 187, 194, 200, 203, 209, 212, 217, 220, 221

Page Swords, 13, 71, 88, 118, 137, 143, 149, 157, 167, 204, 219, 220, 221
Page Wands, 12, 58, 61, 81, 94, 95, 103, 104, 116, 120, 137, 141, 144, 151, 154, 158, 159, 163, 171, 177, 186, 189, 190, 193, 195, 202, 207, 208, 211, 215, 219, 220, 221

Q

Queen Cups, 14, 91, 104, 135, 140, 160, 171, 175, 183, 186, 201, 214, 219, 221
Queen Pentacles, 14, 132, 166, 211
Queen Swords, 13, 61, 64, 86, 90, 129, 137, 148, 168, 169, 195, 215
Queen Wands, 12, 60, 102, 118, 136, 149, 169, 182, 184, 190, 197

S

Star, 12, 73, 78, 96, 107, 125, 151, 169, 176, 182, 216
Strength, 11, 64, 74, 86, 116, 128, 129, 136, 138, 142, 146, 149, 153, 174, 175, 177, 178, 180, 189, 207, 210, 213, 218, 220, 221
Sun, 12, 25, 75, 94, 115, 132, 140, 153, 164, 182, 213, 217

T

Temperance, 11, 70, 110, 142, 148, 161, 193, 194, 213, 217, 218, 220, 221
Tower, 12, 29, 72, 83, 116, 121, 123, 150, 151, 167, 183, 185, 195, 199, 204, 216, 219, 221

W

Wheel of Fortune, 11, 66, 113, 158, 192, 212, 218
World, 6, 12, 77, 88, 101, 118, 126, 133, 155, 167, 168, 170, 180, 191, 196, 199, 214, 216, 220, 221

Printed in Great Britain
by Amazon